No
Other
Foundation

SURE FOUNDATION PUBLISHERS

"...Behold I lay in Zion for a foundation a stone, a tried stone, a precious corner stone, a SURE FOUNDATION:..."

THE ULTIMATES

for 1964-65

First bound edition - 1965
Second bound edition - 1968
Third bound edition - 1975
Fourth bound edition - 1985

Fourth Printing-1985

Printed in U.S.A.

5 6 7—90 89 88 87

No Other Foundation

Published

for

SURE FOUNDATION

Route 2, Box 74
Cloverdale, IN. 46120

The Contents

THE INTRODUCTION

The Foundation, The Footing and The Building

THE ULTIMATE CONCEPTION:

1
Changing and enlarging moods!
How our cast of mind shapes our conceptions.
What it means to change climate and soil!
Consider four kinds of poverty.
By the Cross God moves us into His conception.
What really determines the ultimate conception?

THE ULTIMATE FOUNDATION:

2
Why does a life-work crash or collapse?
Learning to recognize the Foundation.
Are you controlled by the "party spirit"?
Learning how to pull out the rug!

THE ULTIMATE MINISTRY:

3
A ministry of apparent success—or divine increase.
A ministry of death instead of life.
The preaching about the Cross—or of the Cross.
In our ministry—what are we occupied with?
Ministering from a new position.
To participate in this ultimate ministry.
Our ministry is too general—not specific!

THE ULTIMATE PROMOTION:

4
Willing to honestly recognize the lust of position-seeking.
What governs rejection or promotion by the Lord
The source of true honor!

THE ULTIMATE SERVICE:

5

We must consider whether ours is mere service or devotion.
God will be expressive through yielded personality.
When we try to "hardsell" the Gospel.
By what power do you minister?
The testing time of religious foundations.
What is the goal of our service?
If you would serve.

THE ULTIMATE GIVING:

6

No longer in the giving business!
We must also learn to receive.
Three kinds of giving.
What are the laws which should govern our giving?
What is ultimate giving?
Have you discovered this priority in your giving?

THE ULTIMATE PREPARATION:

7

His preparation always builds character.
Professional training or Spirit-wrought preparation.
The difference between shedding or springling of blood.
God does not want your training, He wants you!

THE ULTIMATE PHILOSOPHY:

8

Which one are you?
Beware! Lest you be spoiled!
The Bible is so often improperly used.
Ever learning, yet missing THE TRUTH!
When the Hebrews lived by His revelation.
Consider the characters in this modern controversy.

THE ULTIMATE ISSUE IN LIFE:

9

All creation fulfills His purpose except....!
Life's three-fold secret unfolds.
Designed to express His Life.
He is the Alpha and Omega of our life.
How to fulfill life's highest purpose!
That which is merely related to man—cannot be ultimate!
What is the ultimate issue in life?

The Introduction

THOSE WHO HAVE been reading the journals these past four years will have already "caught" the burden and vision of this writing. However, since many will be starting with this bound series of the 1964-1965 journals, it will be helpful to them if we give a preparatory word as to the meaning of the term *ultimate*.

In this present day when the emphasis in religious circles is on what God has done and can do for man, it is encouraging that an increasing number of people are being awakened to see what God has purposed and desired for Himself. Years ago when we first came into this God-centered viewpoint and began to share it, there seemed to be so very few with an "ear to hear." Now, in these past five years, with the wide-scale ripening of humanism in most religious circles, there has developed a deep disgust in the heart of thinking believers and unbelievers alike.

Almost every day we are amazed how even men of the world, who have no spiritual insight, voice their disgust for the average evangelical believer who seems bent on using God for his own purpose, welfare and blessing. Something woven deep into the moral nature recognizes this is wrong—selfish and warped.

So when we use the term *ultimate* it is to show how everything should be adjusted and related to God for His purpose, pleasure and satisfaction. Instead of man living in his own viewpoint where he interprets and relates all things to himself, it is God who lifts man up into HIS ULTIMATE VIEWPOINT where he can appreciate the glory, wisdom and design of a God-centered universe.

There is, of course, always the concern and fear in some that when God becomes central and all things exist for His pleasure and glory it will seem to push poor man into the shadows where there is seemingly no place or concern for him at all. Nothing could be further from the design and purpose of God! It does not imply that to be God-honoring is to be creature-degrading. Those who are still interpreting from their own human viewpoint are sure to accept this insinuation devised by the Enemy himself. But those who have truly moved up into the Divine viewpoint have always announced: "Oh God, how glorious, beyond words to

7

express, is Thy purpose for Thyself and Thy desire to include man in all its glory." When God truly comes into His own place of glory, then man also comes into that fullest intention of God.

In this present series of journals we are considering three things:
1. The FOUNDATION we are to live upon,
2. THE FOOTING which supports THE FOUNDATION,
3. THE BUILDING which God allows on THE FOUNDATION.

WHAT IS THE FOUNDATION men are to live upon? We must go back to Paul's words to the Corinthians: "According to the grace of God which was given unto me, as a wise masterbuilder I HAVE LAID A FOUNDATION." What was this foundation which Paul declared he had laid? If Paul called himself a wise masterbuilder there is no doubt that he understood what this foundation was; however, he does not himself explain it. Perhaps it is because the Lord Jesus had already made this so clear when He was here. Perhaps it was something which the apostles had already shared as common knowledge throughout the early church. Anyway, we must for an answer turn back to the words of the Lord Jesus as He addresses Simon Peter. Jesus, who never seemed to care what men said or thought about Him, suddenly put the question to His disciples: "Who do men say that I, the Son of Man, am?" Then turning from the views and speculations of others, He went a step further: "Who say ye that I am?" His challenge drew forth spontaneously from Peter the historic confession: *"Thou art the Christ, the Son of the living God."* What a confession from the lips of Peter! As Jesus made clear, Peter's confession was called forth by a God-given revelation. "Flesh and blood hath not revealed it unto thee, but my Father which is in heaven." In explaining the significance of this portion, Watchman Nee has said:

"It is important to understand this passage, for as we shall see, it really defines the point from which, later, Paul in his turn begins. What did Jesus imply? Thou art *Petros*, a little stone—one who is to be builded with others into the basic structure of my Church (see Eph. 2:20; Rev. 21:19)—and on THIS ROCK (petra—speaking of another which is THE ROCK)—I will build. What then is the Church? Is it a structure of living stones founded upon a rock? What is the rock? Here it is that we need to be very clear. *It is a confession based upon a revelation of a Person."* (From WHAT SHALL THIS MAN DO).

What could be more important than understanding this Rock—as THE FOUNDATION upon which God has intended all building. Surely this was no empty confession out from Peter's own point of view. Jesus was using this occasion to emphasize that all spiritual building must be upon

8

this FOUNDATION: i.e. upon the revelation of the Person of Jesus. It is not merely facts about Him or about what He did—but ABOUT WHO HE CHIEFLY IS: Christ, THE SON OF THE LIVING GOD.

Either men have seen this foundation and know its importance or they don't. God has designed that HIS SON shall be the only foundation to support the things men live by. Whatever is established upon Him becomes constant, unmovable and steadfast.

In His days on earth there were so many who followed Christ, who even pressed upon Him and were healed, yet they did not "know Him." Like the throngs today who sit in the church pews every Sunday, they only saw Him with their natural eye. Indeed they saw Him as the answer to all their own needs, but God intended for them to "see" Him as THE FOUNDATION of their life and ministry.

Basically the whole issue is a matter of enlightenment—of revelation from God. Our present religious predicament is simply that men cumber the ground with "other foundations" because they have not really seen THE FOUNDATION. Jesus stated it very clearly when he said that only "the pure in heart shall see...." He meant that only those with a pure motive—those without private ambition, those without any hope of building a personal kingdom—could see by revelation from God. And furthermore, this clear seeing was not to be merely a gate one would pass through, rather it was to be a pathway in which one would walk. Once revelation is past, it may become merely a doctrine or theological tenent; but revelation that is continually present—that is a moment by moment participation in Him; it is something living. Thus we see that this rock which Jesus spoke of was not Peter; nor was it some doctrine. This rock, or foundation, was simply *our confession of the revelation of Him.* Upon this God is building a living church.

THE FOOTING which supports THE FOUNDATION

Now if God intends for His children to live by continuous participation in His Son, and if this living revelation is THE FOUNDATION of our spiritual life and building, we must go a bit deeper to consider the FOOTING upon which this all important foundation rests. Any wise masterbuilder knows that many seemingly good foundations give way because they lack a proper footing.

What is this FOOTING? We must not only understand how the Eternal Father is this proper footing, but we must appreciate the importance of Him as the ultimate footing for all revelation. Just what do we mean by this? One can quickly detect from the present religious scene that many are being sidetracked by various and sundry revelations. It is quite popular these days to have a new revelation for every meeting. And there are those who will be quick to acknowledge: "Oh yes, we live by new revelations all the time." Yet this is just the snare! It is exactly what we are hoping to discern and expose. The Father is very jealous that we have *one* revelation—OF HIS LOVELY SON, not many revelations regarding good and important things. We are to see HIM as everything God designs to share.

In these days some have camped around the "revelation of love" as the all-important thing. So they magnify love. Others have built camp around some revelation of new knowledge which seems to eclipse all else on their horizon. However right or proper it may be, they have made "it" to be their camping place—not HIM. Still others insist they have seen that life is the primary substance of everything in the universe. So, with their new-found revelation they have built camp around another "it"—but yet missed HIM who is intended to be THE REVELATION.

Are These Foundations?

LOVE	LIGHT	LIFE

Please be careful to grasp what I am trying to say. None of these— love, light or life—is really a sufficient foundation for building. If there is anything started, it will simply become a following around some aspect of Him—not Him. However good these revelations may seem, God has designed to give ONE REVELATION—the revelation of HIS SON. Anything else must be seen simply as an outflow of Him. We must see Christ as our life, Christ as our light (knowledge) and Christ as our love.

What we are saying is this: Peter saw the revelation of who Jesus chiefly is; not a Savior, Servant, Lord, Ruler, Healer; not merely life, light or love. No—Christ, the anointed One was before, above and beyond all else THE SON OF THE LIVING GOD. Thus, it is when we see that the Father is before, above and beyond all else that He is, THE FATHER, then we shall see why all revelation centers in who Christ chiefly is: THE SON.

We can now more fully appreciate how the Father is THE FOOTING for this glorious foundation. It is the Father who purposes for His Son to be central in all His economy. Just as the footing is not visible to the eye and we only see the foundation, so the Father is not seen but He has sent forth the Son whom we see. Just as we know a son must have a father; so a foundation must have a footing.

We can realize why the Father is very jealous for His Son. He will not allow any other foundation than the revelation of His Son. Any other revelation than the Person of His lovely Son will distract from Him. He is to have the pre-eminence. Upon Him, and only Him are all things to be summed up. Finally we must see . . .

THE ONLY BUILDING WHICH GOD ALLOWS ON THE FOUNDATION

As we have pictured, everyone who learns to live by revelation will know an inner enlargement and development in footing, foundation and building. As he plumbs new depths of God the Father there will be an enlargement of footing; as he discovers how the Son is actually everything in life, there will be a real development of foundation in the inner life; as Christ is built into the inner fabric it will be evident that only He is material for spiritual building.

The Inner determines the Outer

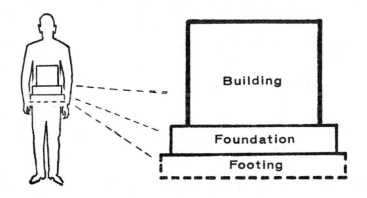

Accordingly our whole ministry changes. We must realize that there can never be any greater ministry outwardly than what has been wrought within our innerman. If there is a proper footing laid in us, then we will produce that footing in our ministry unto others. If there is a proper foundation laid in us, then we will produce that foundation in others. If there is a proper spiritual building going up in us, then we will produce that same building in others. Our outward ministry is actually the reflection of our inner life.

Paul seemed to understand this principle when he wrote to the Corinthians. We have quoted his statement: "I have laid a foundation." Now he continues by saying, "But any man who builds on the foundation using as his material gold, silver, precious stones, wood, hay, or stubble, must know that each man's work will one day be shown for what it is" (1 Cor. 3:10).

God may allow our life-work to stand momentarily, but He will not allow anything to remain on THE FOUNDATION which is not proper building material. I can almost hear Him saying to some of those who are now building, "You may spend your whole life on that, but it will all go up in smoke. It is not suitable building material; it is not something of Christ which I have wrought by the Spirit into lives."

What is this wood, hay and stubble which God will not allow as building material? One may look at pastors who have spent years in gathering people in their congregation. To the visible eye it looks like something has been done. Yet God sees the human energies of man without the help of the Spirit and announces: "This is just a pile of boards. I cannot accept them unless they are over-laid with gold. And this over-laying is not of man, but a work of the Spirit." God is forced to announce: "Have I not told you I cannot have this on my Foundation for it is something wrought of man. It is too earthy. I must have gold which I have wrought through pressure, through fire, through purifying."

Again, we have seen men build knowledge, doctrine, theology into people. Yet in the hour of real pressure all this which has not been translated into reality will not hold them. It is like hay and stubble they have been feeding upon, and this can never nourish the inner man nor become building material for God. Recently I heard a brother, who had been an outstanding Bible teacher for 15 years, share the deepest confession of his heart: "All I have known has only puffed me up, but it has not built me up in the inner life. Outwardly I am a builder, but inwardly I am a shambles. I, myself, have been feeding upon mere hay and feeding it to others."

Finally, as you approach these journals I have this prayer: "Lord, please do not let any of this knowledge be merely for the mind, but may it pass through into the spirit as revelation for the inner man; may it bring such a revolution in foundational conceptions as to rectify the life and ministry of all those who read so that our God may reap untold fruit for Himself."

THE

ULTIMATE

CONCEPTION

DISCOVERING YOUR
PREVAILING MOOD

OUR CAST OF MIND
SHAPES OUR CONCEPTIONS

BY THE CROSS GOD MOVES US
INTO HIS CONCEPTION

WHAT REALLY DETERMINES
THE ULTIMATE CONCEPTION?

Changing

and

enlarging

moods

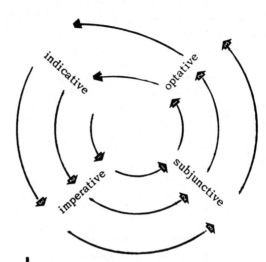

IN BEGINNING THIS JOURNAL it is important that you learn to detect your own mood—for you do have a prevailing mood. As you approach anything new, there is always one mood which prevails, and like a pair of glasses colors or determines what you see. It is also true that moods tend to change and move in an enlarging cycle. Frequently they have been depicted in the four moods of the Greek verb: indicative, imperative, subjunctive and optative.

Let us consider how you passed through various moods:

Do you remember your first days as a new convert, when you had just experienced passing from "death unto Life?" You started in the *indicative* mood. Like the Apostle John, this was your testimony: "...that which we have heard, that which we have seen with our eyes, that which we beheld and our hands handled concerning the Word of Life...declare we unto you...that ye may have fellowship with us." Yes, you were declaring to everyone that all things were new, vibrant and thrilling.

Later this initial mood (the indicative) gave way to the *imperative* mood in which you attempted to thrust upon others that which had become so vital, so imperative in your own life and walk as a believer. What was at first a joyful declaring soon became virtual demanding. In your increasing zeal and over-anxiety you passed from the indicative to the imperative mood. Since this mood always meets with rebuff and indifference, you were soon brought into disappointment and discouragement.

Thus, you pass into the third mood, the subjunctive which brings about some inward questioning and reservation. With these tossing winds and inward pressures your roots begin to go down. You become more cautious, more quizical, more deliberate. You cannot understand your own mood. Everything which was once so joyfully declared, in an almost glibe manner, and so positively demanded is now being re-evaluated. It

15

seems like a perilous hour, but it is inevitable. Borrowed concepts are becoming built-in concepts.

So the *subjunctive* mood, in the normal course, will usually give way to the *optative* mood. In this new mood you have become expectant, and hopeful. You start searching the horizon for some glimmer of truth or reality which will usher in a new era in your life. At this point you live with all the scars and accumulative effects of the past, yet you look hopefully to the future and so the cycle starts over again. Surely as you have reached this new phase, there is a combination of the past moods with their mark upon you. But your earnest quest for some new liberating truth will become the doorway into another plane, and thence you pass into the indicative mood again.

Let us remember, just as children and young people pass through these cycles in their maturing, so adults go through (or ought to) these phases. I say *ought to,* because sometime there are those who get stalled in a certain phase too long and it warps their outlook and conceptions in life. And what is true of individuals is often true of corporate groups. We have observed how congregations either pass through these various moods or get stalled. In a broader sense even historic Christianity has seemed to pass through this cycle since its first century founding.

THE CHANGING COURSE OF HISTORY.

It would seem, if the larger cycle of history means anything, that we are even now passing through an inward groaning—a sort of "spiritual travail" in preparation for giving birth to a "new age." Ten years ago when we first began to share the "seeds of ultimate truth" which were beginning to break upon our heart, there was only small evidence of hunger or interest. Today it is quite different. Crisis after crisis has produced a fast ripening. Amid the terrifying world conditions there is now a deep-seated frustration and disillusionment throughout the Church. It is almost as with a single voice that God's children are calling out: "Oh God...is there not *something* which will answer our desperate plight?" Truly men in vast numbers are awakening to the optative mood. There is a strange expectancy on every hand.

As you read these pages remember that your present mood, like a pair of glasses, will determine your sense of appreciation or your ability to discern the value and necessity of certain concepts being shared. It is our deepest conviction that today the Lord's people need the recovery of the Paternal approach; that is, seeing all that the Father has purposed for Himself through His lovely Son and how by the Holy Spirit's working we are gloriously related to that ultimate intention. Until there is a recovery of the God-centered outlook, approach, philosophy and central theme of the Bible, there can be no ultimate conceptions.

We do not overlook our own mood as we write. In the past three years since these journals have been sent throughout the world, we, too, have passed from the joyful declaration of ultimate truths into the imperative

16

mood. We have observed how pastors and leaders have been revolutionized in their thinking and ministry. We sense the urgency of the hour and
it almost causes us to demand men to turn from their surface truths to
consider that which seems to us of such imperative importance. There is
also the awareness Jeremiah must have had, that one cannot do much
solid building or planting until there has first been a "... rooting out,
pulling down, destroying and throwing down..." of all that is human-
istic, man-centered and God-dishonoring.

Finally, will you pray with us that His Body shall be prospered and
built up? We seek no private faction or separate movement. We must be
continually related to that main-stream of the Church which God Himself,
has watched over and protected unto this hour. We look with eager expectancy to see how God will use ultimate truths to mature, empower,
envision and enlarge His present program of recovery. So, we find ourselves being gripped by a combination of the indicative, the imperative,
the subjunctive and the optative moods. It is hoped that the reader is
likewise sensitive to his enlarging moods.

Check yourself! How far have you advanced ?

1 *In the first mood* you become a Christian. You are a new-born
babe just discovering some of the fundational truths of the Bible.
You enjoy a great hunger and a tremendous receptivity; everything tastes good and looks appetizing; you just can't seem to
get enough spiritual food.

2 *In the second mood* you become desirous of imposing your new
discoveries and wonderful liberating truth upon others. Because
you know what it has done for you, you realize how imperative
these things are; however your zeal and enthusiasm begins to
meet with resistance in others.

3 *In the third mood* you begin to realize how some things which
excited you were more knowledge than reality. And you begin to
react. Negative attitudes begin to hold sway. Some of the things
which looked so good, need to come into sharper focus; others
things which you now discover were not right make you a little
bitter and you tend to be over-cautious.

4 *In the fourth mood* you move beyond the critical, cautious attitude and there is a hopeful, expectant mood. So you have passed
from the open, through the demanding, through the quizical into
the hopeful mood. Your mood brings you to this frame of mind:
"... maybe here is something I have not heretofore encountered;
maybe here is something I should give careful consideration to,
for it might just be God's way of answering the cry and yearning
of my heart." And when you have found that new truth you are
ready once again to start the cycle all over.

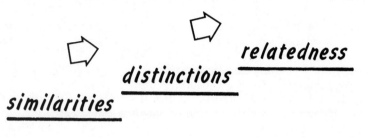

similarities → distinctions → relatedness

HOW OUR CAST OF MIND SHAPES
OUR CONCEPTIONS

IT IS MARVELLOUS THAT GOD has giv-
en each of us a built-in mechanism by
which we learn to discern. As we have pictured in the diagram there are
three phases through which we pass again and again. First we recognize similarities, next distinctions and later we move on to see the relatedness of things. It is not only as little children or adolescents that
we must le: rn likenesses, differences and relatedness, but in a sense
our whole life is a process of continuous learning. The problem is this:
after moving through several planes there is often a certain bent or cast
in our mentality which begins to prevail. When we get stalled in one
phase—when we begin emphasizing only likenesses—we over-develop
the poetic cast of mind, or we begin emphasizing only distinctions—and
we over-develop the scientific cast of mind, or we begin emphasizing
only relatedness/and we over-develop the philosophic cast of mind
In one of his illuminating editorials, the late A. W. Tozer wrote

> Wherever men think and try to express their thoughts
> two types of mind are clearly revealed, the scientific
> and the poetic. I mean not that all men are either poets
> or scientists; I mean rather that the cast of mind that
> makes a poet is marked in some men while others have
> a bent distinctly scientific. The one may never write
> poetry nor the other engage in scientific pursuits; but
> the bent is there.
>
> The scientist is concerned with differences, the
> poet with likenesses. The poet may see the world in a

grain of sand; the scientist is more concerned with the number and composition of the grains of sand in the world. I believe not only that this difference is among men, but within each man. In every one of us there is somewhat of both scientist and poet until one gains the ascendancy and crowds the other out. Then we have a man bent only on analysis or a man incapable of analysis, a man altogether scientist or altogether poet—that is, only half a man.

Unfortunately this controversy between the poet and the scientist among men and within each man is found also in the field of religion. The Church of Christ has not escaped the conflict but has been pulled and torn by the play of these contrary forces. Strong leaders have risen to stamp their images upon whole denominations for centuries, and the body of believers has divided where the leaders differed. In one group certain truths have been ignored or suppressed to make greater room for other truths that were felt to be more important; in another the same thing has taken place with an opposite set of truths, and serious cleavage has been the result.

Those who insist upon seeing the world in a grain of sand have their slavish, unthinking followers, and those who go doggedly about the task of counting the grains of sand in the world have theirs. The moral texture and spiritual complexion of the two groups are so completely different from each other than an uninformed but intelligent person who might chance to spend some time with each group could be forgiven for concluding that they drew their beliefs from different Bibles or perhaps even worshiped different gods.

It is quite evident that much of the division among God's children springs out of these over-developed casts of mind. In the church we have the preacher who tends toward the poetic cast of mind, the teacher who tends toward the scientific cast, and the prophet who tends toward the philosophic cast of mind. Each of these, without realizing it, may gather his own kind under his wing. "Birds of a similar cast of mind tend to flock together."

With the preacher there is that tendency to generalize or over-simplify; by a single wave of the poetic wand he can diagnose every problem. But the teacher who delves into the differing causes will insist upon a depth analysis. Too often dissention is invited by those who insist upon hair-splitting definitions and interpretations. Then there is the prophet who lives with the long-range view. His tendency to over-look the practical side of life will create no little irritation among those with a different cast of mind.

Perhaps it would be helpful for the reader to evaluate his own tendencies. Make a check in front of the statements which best describe your prevailing cast of mind.

CONCEPTIONS ARE SHAPED BY OUR PREVAILING MENTALITY

_____ Do you tend to generalize in your statements? After reading a book would your typical statement be, "I'm sure I could never understand anything that author would ever write"?

_____ Do you tend to over use such words as *all, never* and *only?*

_____ Do you enjoy broad outlines more than minute details?

_____ Do you emphasize the panoramic bird's-eye view rather than a close scrutinizing of any part? If so, these traits would explain it is the *poetic* which is prevailing in your mentality.

_____ Do you tend to enjoy technicalities, to specialize in details, to be very explicit in your speaking? Then you would be quite precise by saying: "There is an occasional statement in that book which I did not grasp."

_____ Do you particularly tend toward a mystical interpretation or enjoy the fresh breath of poetic expression? Or instead, would you bury your nose in heavy, exacting reading? If so, these traits would explain it is the *scientific* which is prevailing in your mentality.

_____ Do you tend to deal with the abstract rather than the concrete in expressing yourself; you like to day-dream; to take many a jaunt to yonder lofty isle? There you can live beyond time in the splendor of eternity. Instead of bothering with mere similarities or distinctions, you would emphasize the over-all relatedness of everything in the universe.

_____ Does it become quite trying to you when friends seem to be unduly occupied with mere parts when you know that first of all they should recognize the whole? If so, it is the *philosophic* which is prevailing in your mentality.

WHAT IT MEANS:
TO CHANGE CLIMATE AND SOIL!

I STOOD looking at a shallow dish of water in which some kernels of corn were breaking and sending forth green shoots. In that moment something I had been trying to express came into mind so vividly. It was just as though the Lord were saying: "It is not nature's design for kernels to remain in this dish. Even so, I have too many little babes like these sprouting kernels who are under the delusion that, having accepted Me as their personal Saviour, all they need to do is grow. They do not seem to realize there can only be spiritual growth as there is proper climate and proper soil."

I pondered what it would mean to be placed in a proper climate. He seemed to say: "Your climate is like a framework—so very important. There are some frameworks in which it is impossible to grow. If life is bounded by the narrow framework of an earthly existence ending in the narrower framework of a coffin, then, of course, a stunted life is guaranteed; you will have the same limitations as that kernel which remains in the dish. Moreover, if gaining a place in heaven by and by is your only goal, then you cannot expect spiritual growth, for there is no proper climate; you can only expect to reach heaven because Another has paid your admission price.

But if life holds the possibility of an infinite growth after the Infinite Pattern, then that should focus your eyes, stir your heart and quicken your spirit, for you can live with real expectancy for the big, the significant, the ultimate. Until you have been awakened to this kind of goal, do not assume that you have begun to breathe of that Eternal Climate."

I understood the importance of a proper climate, now—what was the proper soil? Then I remembered a verse that is often quoted at this point as the answer: "But go on growing in the *grace* and *knowledge* of our Lord and Saviour, Jesus Christ." The way people have used this verse has always troubled me! So often they seem to assume that you can begin to grow from where you are. But you don't grow "into grace," or "into knowledge."

As I looked again at the little kernels in which death and decay was working, yet in which life was sprouting forth, I realized the importance of being transferred into "another dish"—into the environment or soil of His grace. As long as the little kernel remained in the dish, it was still living from its own stored up nutrients. Similarly, as long as there is no changing of the center of my life *from self to God,* there can be no real growth, or living by Him as my new source of Life. Living on the soil of myself, I simply cannot grow.

We are not made to grow as a self-centered being—living in a display dish. We all have witnessed young converts who seemed to suddenly blossom forth in a burst of life and religious activity. But alas, the hour of withering and drooping! What an awakening when they discover that such was not spiritual growth, but merely the development of their inner soul-powers. Like the kernel of corn, they were still "in the dish"—living out from their own self-center; therefore they could not long endure the real blasts of persecution.

We are designed to grow as our roots are in HIM. Hence the very first step in growing spiritually is a transplanting—a shifting from a self-centered to a God-centered source of life: this is growing in grace. And further, we must become alive and completely harmonized in the climate of His desire and purpose: this is growing in knowledge.

How all this cuts across a great deal of modern emphasis which would find all the answers within yourself! Discover yourself, cultivate yourself, express yourself-these are the slogans. And for awhile this emphasis works. It gives you a shot in the arm of positive assertion and turns you away from negativism. So far so good! But only "so far." Beyond that initial boost it cannot go. Living in one's own soul-soil, resources are very quickly exhausted. So the aspirant in self-discovery, self-cultivation and self-expression turns to another cult for another "shot." The soil of self was never intended to be the seed-bed of eternal values.

A lady, very proper in appearance and outlook, who never talked to God except in the language of the King James Version, heard Christ saying to her in a service one afternoon: "This isn't for you. Come outside, I want to talk with you." She protested that she would have to climb over three people, one of them her husband, to get out, and they would consider her ill and unbalanced. His Voice persisted. So she went out.

In murmuring she pondered: "But suppose He wouldn't be there when I got out there?" He was there! And insisted, "Let's take a walk."

They went up the hill to the chapel. There He seemed to impel her to pull out of her inner life, resentments and self-centeredness and lay them before Him. She was ashamed and said limply: "What shall I do?" "Suppose we have a funeral right here," He replied. And they did! She discovered what it meant to change climate—and to change soil. She saw herself buried with Christ, but also raised to a newness of life. SHE WAS PLANTED INTO A NEW SOIL. Now her roots were in Him instead

22

of in herself. When they walked down the hill there was evidence all over her face. Instead of being a wild flower, she was as a lovely flower breathing a new climate with roots LIVING IN HIM.

I think sometimes we will be covered with shame when we meet the Lord Jesus and realize how blind and ignorant we were when He brought people to us who needed help. So often we intruded into their lives; we tried to find out what was wrong. But that should not be our first concern. Our first business is to pray and counsel them to turn toward Him, so that when their awakening comes, Jesus Christ will be the first One they meet. Then, they will immediately get their roots into Him as their source instead of depending on us. The one who meets a soul in the hour of its awakening has the opportunity of making or marring that soul.

Too often we have, so to speak, turned them into "dish" Christians. In their increasing dependence upon us for a "watering" they could hardly move beyond their narrow framework of the little display dish. Growth is *unto their own blessing* not *unto Him*. Have we not, at times, seen a whole group or congregation become so dependent upon their pastor or teacher that they never develop their own roots in the Lord Jesus. Therefore the whole church becomes simply a lovely display dish—living unto itself.

It is quite imperative that God should break whatever "dish" confines or limits us. And this is what happens so often as He begins to shake lives that they may be settled on something unshakeable. Only as our roots go down into Him can there be expansion in our heart and....

PREPARATION TO ACCEPT THESE ENLARGING CONCEPTIONS.

LIFE has one passion and purpose: Bringing honor, glory and satisfaction.....

In Him I died...to become alive...

unto Him

His death provides victorious life...

unto God

Jesus died....

for me

for me

WHICH ONE OF THESE FOUR MEN IS REPRESENTATIVE OF YOU?

1

I represent more than half of the world population who lives in dire poverty. How can I help but court an inner bitterness toward those who have been blessed merely because of their place of birth or because of circumstances they are wholly unresponsible for? Would it not seem to everyone that *life has been against me?* I've never really had a chance to choose anything but poverty. I am a victim! POVERTY HAS BEEN IMPOSED UPON ME!

2

I represent that portion of humanity who has enjoyed sufficient material things which, if they could, should have brought happiness and contentment. So I continue my pursuit of grasping for more of this world and its pleasure, yet inwardly I know I am lacking in wisdom, even in the ability to enjoy or appreciate things. Yes, lacking in that thing most needful: finding the true meaning and purpose of life. It is all too evident that I have not discovered the built-in laws of God's economy. Therefore I AM REAPING RETRIBUTIVE POVERTY.

CONSIDER FOUR KINDS OF POVERTY

IS IT NOT STRANGE that intelligent men will declare war on poverty, yet hardly attempt to distinguish between the different kinds of poverty—whether imposed, retributive, ascetic or planned? In this Western world we are so gripped by the god of materialism we can hardly recognize any kind other than material poverty. However, in the Eastern world where most of the emphasis has been upon "spiritual" values, people are beginning to recognize their double bankruptcy—both spiritual and material. What an hour of challenge! How can we convince the world, both East and West, that there is a reality in Christ they have not yet experienced. Mere talking, or more writing will not! God is calling those who have entered into life in the Spirit to become living exhibits; those who have moved into HIS VIEWPOINT will gladly embrace "planned poverty" as a way to greater fruitfulness. Don Hillis has described some of those in days past who embraced that way.

3

I represent that smaller portion of humanity who has recognized that things can never satisfy. Like cinders in the grate, they only clog the system and dull the real powers of man. With King Solomon I have come to cry out: "All is vanity." Now in my rejection of material things I am pursuing that true wealth which I have hoped would come by the development of the inner man. Yet strangely, in all my self-denial and sacrifice I must confess that I am still oh-so-poor in my inner man. Could it be that I have but imposed material poverty on myself and am only reaping retributive poverty in my inner man? Oh what a farce! —if MY ASCETIC POVERTY IS FOR NAUGHT.

4

I represent that very small remnant among men who have found HIS secret for fulness of life: "...though he was rich, yet for your sakes He became poor, that ye through His poverty might be rich." Hence, my goal is not to pursue happiness in things, neither to find it by the development of the inner man. Since I have been turned from grasping and self-relating, my goal in living is to be *fruitful unto God*, to satisfy Him." For one who has entered into such life, actually there is no poverty—only fullness. Until one has come to live in THIS VIEWPOINT he cannot distinguish between ascetic poverty and THAT WHICH IS PLANNED POVERTY.

THE JOY OF EMBRACING "PLANNED POVERTY"

WILLIAM CAREY, the consecrated cobbler-turned-missionary, gave $499,000 to missions during his years as a servant of the Lord in India. How did he do it? Carey went to the mission field with a salary of $250 a year. While in India he was hired by the government to teach in a university at $7,500 a year. Carey continued to live on $250, giving the rest to the work of the Lord. That was planned poverty.

As a youth, John Wesley began working for $150 a year. He gave $10 to the Lord. His salary was doubled the second year, but Wesley continued to live on $140, giving $160 to Christian work. During his third year, Wesley received $600. He kept $140 while $460 were given to the Lord. That was planned poverty.

Robert Atherton, who was raised in luxury, gave $5,000,000 to the work of the Lord. He did not do it without sacrificial living. A letter received from a missionary in China read, 'Were I in England again, I would gladly live in one room, make the floor my bed, a box my chair, another my table, rather than that the heathen should perish for lack of a knowledge of Christ.' Atherton followed these suggestions almost to the letter for the rest of his life.

William Borden died before his twenty-sixth birthday. He had given his entire fortune of $25,000,000 to the work of the Lord before going out as a missionary. That was purposeful poverty.

And what about Moses who rejected the name, the fame, the power, and the wealth of Egypt, only to suffer affliction with the children of Israel? His choice was premeditated. He esteemed the reproach of Christ greater riches than the treasures in Egypt.

We are told concerning the churches and Macedonia that—

'in most difficult circumstances, their joy and the fact of being down to their last penny themselves produced a magnificent concern for other people. I can guarantee that they were willing to give to the limit of their means, yes, beyond their means, without the slightest urging from me or anyone else.

'In fact, they simply begged us to accept their gifts and so let them share in the honor of supporting their brothers in Christ. Nor was their gift, as I must confess I had expected, a mere cash payment. Instead, they made a complete dedication of themselves, first to the Lord, and then to us as God's appointed ministers' (2 Cor. 8:2-5, Phillips translation).

One wonders if it was not the sacrificial spirit of Paul which inspired the deliberate and dedicated frugality of the churches in Macedonia. Paul's walk with God was one of planned poverty. He counted all personal profit but refuse in the light of eternity.

Paul in turn walked in the footsteps of his Master who *'though he was rich, yet for our sakes ...became poor that we through his poverty might be made rich.'* The planned poverty in which our Lord lived was deliberate and purposeful. There was nothing hasty or unconsidered about it. The plan was conceived from before the foundation of the world. The purpose was that we might enjoy eternal riches. How great was that sacrifice and how deep the poverty only heaven will reveal.

In the bright light of our Lord's example, we dare not allow our giving to grow out of the shallow ground of spasmodic emotional stirrings. There must be something deep, deliberate, and disciplined about true stewardship. The work of the Lord cannot thrive on the fringe benefits of our income. Poverty stricken souls who are without hope and without God will never enter into the riches of grace in Christ apart from planned poverty in the lives of God's children.

Is our Lord worthy of anything less than planned poverty on our part? Are the souls for whom He died deserving of anything less than that sacrifice which will enable them to hear the gospel of His love? The manger is planned poverty." DON HILLIS   The Missionary Broadcaster

26

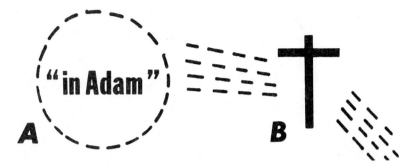

BY THE CROSS GOD
MOVES US INTO HIS CONCEPTION

IT IS ALMOST IMPOSSIBLE to hide our predicament! Every church I know about (with any measure of life) is plagued with problems. Our conceptions are just too small, too inadequate and too limited. We have allowed our natural attitudes, moods, mentality and makeup to warp or shape our conceptions. God's remedy is to take all that is natural to the Cross. He can neither revise or revamp them, for they issue out of the soul-life of the Adam-man. Through a union with Christ in His death and burial, we can rise to a wholly new sphere of life. Old conceptions begin to pass away and *all conceptions become new.*

OUR GREAT NEED IS THIS: we must not only know the doctrine that we died and rose again with Christ, but we must also know in experience that by the Cross, death has been applied to our natural moods, mentality and makeup. Paul exhorts the Colossians that, "... ye have put off the old (Adam) man ... and have put on the new man which is renewed in knowledge ... " Too long we have been content to quote, "I have been crucified with Christ ... ", yet we have managed to escape the reality of this. As proof of this we need only refer to the four problems presented at the beginning of this article. It is not liberal, modernistic churches that we are speaking of, rather it is those who pride themselves as evangelistic, fundamental, Bible believing churches who love to sing and teach about the Cross, yet by-pass its reality.

A illustrates all men "in Adam" as they live unto themselves. Attempting to be "ultimate", man seeks to use God and all His works for his own end. Now this self-relating is the one reason why our natural moods, mentality and makeup gets us into so much trouble. All our conceptions are warped for we see and interpret through colored glasses which have "self" as the center and object of interest.

So a person who, either consciously or subconsciously, starts out to make the universe revolve around him will live in a false universe that

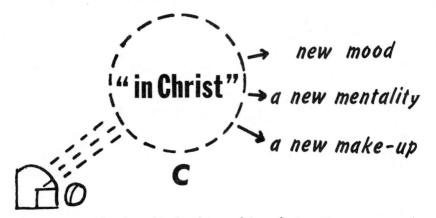

new mood

a new mentality

a new make-up

C

is sure to tumble about his head in awful confusion. Man was never intended to be the center or to shape his own conceptions. So let us consider how God has made provision for man to move out of his little selfish world of warped moods, mentality and makeup into God-centeredness.

B illustrates how God, through the Cross and by His Son, has put an end to the old universe of which man seeks to be the center. Paul gives a brief survey of this in 2 Cor. 5:14, 15, "... we thus judge, that one died for all, therefore all died; and he died for all, that they which live should no longer live unto themselves, but unto Him who for their sakes died and rose again."

When God looks down upon the Cross He sees that we are united in death with His Son. He reckons that the source of soulish moods, mentality and makeup is henceforth cut off. Now as we rise from the grave in Christ, the old source has been exchanged for a NEW SOURCE: CHRIST BECOMES OUR LIFE. He is our new mood, mentality and makeup.

The great tragedy is that while many loudly acclaim this doctrine of union in death with Christ and glory in this new position in Christ, yet the reality of it is not daily expressed in their life and ministry. There are too many who have come forth from the tomb who still wear the garments of the old life. Like Lazarus, when he came from the grave, they need to be loosed from their old bondages and fetters. So we must consider what it really means to live "in Christ" where old things have indeed passed away and all conceptions have become new.

illustrates how man has moved into a new position where he lives in God's viewpoint and conception. Paul explains this new world of spiritual reality in chapters 3,4, and 5 of 2 Corinthians.

OUR NEW MOOD: If Paul had not learned the sufficiency of the Holy Spirit, he would surely have fainted. But he has boldness to announce: "Not that we are sufficient of ourselves to think anything as of ourselves; but our sufficiency is of God; Who hath made us able ministers of the new testament..." Here is the secret. To serve in this NEW MOOD is to have a continual freshness and newness of spirit (Rom 7:6). There is hardly one who ministers who has not sensed failure, deadness and bewilderment. One cannot avoid deep scars as he passes through the various moods—but both scars and moods are left in death.

Under the dominion of the Holy Spirit, one's own spirit is so mingled and cooperative with God's Spirit that he lives with a new freshness and buoyancy. God alone can give this new mood. Therefore Paul could say: "Therefore seeing we have *this ministry*, as we have received mercy (i.e. a new position and living union), we faint not " (2 Cor. 4:1).

OUR NEW MENTALITY: In chapter 4 Paul explains how we are set free from the hidden things of dishonesty, craftiness or deceitfulness. When we are living and serving in the spirit, we are not under the dominion of our reasoning, our thinking, or our point of view. How important this is to the proper life and unity of the Church. Paul indicates how he was troubled on every side, yet not distressed; perplexed, but not in despair. Surely he was confronted with those theologians who always wanted to argue over doctrine. How perplexing! yet Paul said he was not in despair. If we serve according to our knowledge or logic, our mentality or point of view—we will most surely come to despair.

Paul's secret was to be always *in the spirit*, not *in the mind*. To be critical or argumentative is something in the mentality. We can argue doctrine all the time—for a whole year or a lifetime and get nowhere. The more we live out from the soul(ish) source of reasoning or mentality the more we must draw from the old source. But, when we have moved into that living union—into that new position, we can rejoice. All we need say to those who insist upon arguing is, "Lord, I don't know whether I have my dependence upon my natural mind or not, but I do know that Thou art a Spirit living and dwelling in my spirit. I choose to serve Thee *in the spirit*. I refuse to argue with or belittle one who does not live in God's conception."

OUR NEW MAKEUP: We have seen how the sentence of death rests upon our natural mood and crosses out our own mentality. In 2 Cor. 5:14 Paul explains our new makeup. It is neither our head nor our heart—but His overmastering love that constrains. Once our proneness was to judge everything or feel everything after the flesh. We even knew Christ after the flesh. But henceforth we know Him neither in a sentimental, soulish love (that sings about Jesus in a romantic way), nor in a cold, calculated, rationalistic manner. We have now entered into a living union with Christ by which we share His love and His mind. Our new makeup is beyond description: we are indeed a new specie, a wholly new creation of God.

Thus we have seen how passing through the Cross will mean the end to our natural mood, mentality and makeup. This is no mere doctrine, it is a living experience. It is God's way of moving us into His *ultimate conception.*

In this journal we have considered how our passing moods and our built-in mentality shape our conceptions. Our prejudices and selfishness will also shape and color every conception until the Cross has wrought a drastic change. But there is one thing which—above all else—really determines our ultimate conception.

WHERE HE STANDS

or

WHAT HE LOOKS AT

or

WHAT HE IS

LET US SEE which of these three things is the basic determining factor in shaping our conceptions. Consider the shepherd boy, David, as he stands on the hillsides of Palestine watching his flock of sheep. As he looks into the starry heavens he meditates: "When I consider thy heavens, the work of thy fingers, the moon and the stars, which thou hast ordained; what is man that thou art mindful of him and the son of man, THAT THOU VISITEST HIM?" What really inspired and shaped these lofty conceptions of this shepherd boy?

Would any other Jewish lad standing on the hills of Palestine, looking into the heavens, ponder such thoughts about God and His caring for man enough to visit earth? Suppose he were a young lad in Egypt being schooled in the astrology of that day. Then he could not have enjoyed the favored Jewish heritage nor imbibed the climate of God-consciousness which had been so manifest in Israel for centuries. Indeed, standing and looking out upon God's vast heavenly handiwork through a Jewish consciousness would certainly shape and mold his conceptions. We conclude there was something quite important in where David stood and what he looked at, yet aside from this he was still quite distinct from other Jewish shepherd boys. Above all else there seems to be in David—in his makeup, in his heart and inner conditioning —a very special preparation and receptivity toward God. *Where he stood* and *what he looked at* did shape David's conceptions, but there was one thing more basic and primary: *what he was* in his inner being, controlled every other conception.

As I write this, commentator Paul Harvey, has excitedly announced to his radio audience that our space searchers have just recognized a brilliant light now reaching the outer circumference of our universe. Now visible to the most powerful telescope, this light in its activity, seems so completely out of the ordinary; it defies all laws and principles of astronomy; astounding is the only word to describe it!

Immediately we long to penetrate the heavenlies, but we are so limited. Only those scientists at Mt. Palomar can adjust the focus of their telescope upon this new phenomena. They have a decided and a unique advantage. However, God has given to all of us the built-in power to visualize things we can never see with our naked eye. We can closely approximate this seeing with our mind's eye.

Yet once again we should see how our inner being often acts like a sieve to sift every mental conception. Consider how the scientist, who tends to be antagonistic toward God and divine revelation, will make every effort to explain this light as just another natural occurrence in the heavens. Another scientist who is quite neutral and nominal in his religious faith, will likely ask his pastor if there just could be any prophetic significance in this amazing discovery. But the Christian scientist, who is a devout student of prophecy or eschatology, will be prone to cast the rigid scientific approach aside in every effort to prove this brilliant light to be the morning star heralding the return visit of Jesus Christ to this earth. Finally, for those of us who can only visualize, because we have no Mt. Palomar telescope, there is a new spring of hope and a deep longing that surely this is that Holy City finishing its long pilgrimage to this planet. We become excited in anticipation of the glorious age soon to be ushered in! Thus it is not *where we stand* or *what we look at*, but primarily *what we are* in our inner being which governs our conception.

Finally, let us take a big move away from earth, away from time and space, way back into the eternity past. We are standing with God in the eternal NOW, before that first morning hour of creation, before any beginning of creative activity. Here we stand with God the Father looking out of His eyes. We discover it is not the Son who originates the eternal purpose, nor is the Holy Spirit initiating any plans. It is the Eternal Father who is the First Cause and Initiator.

All that we have said up to this point has prepared our thinking to appreciate what really determines the ultimate conception of all conceptions. We have moved away from man and his conceptions; we are in the very heart of God the Father, and are transferred into His ultimate framework of conceptions. In the fullness of His blazing light we discover it is what the Eternal Father is in His *being* and *nature* that

WHAT HE IS IN HIS INNER BEING!

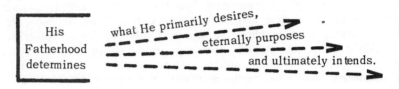

His Fatherhood determines — what He primarily desires, eternally purposes and ultimately intends.

determines His conceptions. Because He is before, above and beyond all else a Life-giving Father, we recognize that His Fatherhood governs what He primarily desires, eternally purposes and ultimately intends. WHAT ELSE COULD A FATHER DESIRE THAN A VAST FAMILY OF CHILDREN LIKE HIMSELF.

So we stand with the Eternal Father on the veranda of the celestial spanse, looking out across the milleniums to that final hour of consummation. We marvel at His omniscient power to visualize the things that are not as though they are. In the eternal NOW He sees the end as well as the beginning. And what is He looking at? What else would a Father heart long for but a VAST FAMILY OF SONS! Then in pointing to His Eternally Begotten Son at His side, the Father announces, "I want everyone of them to be just like HIM, conformed to His very image and likeness." And He continues, "Yes, I can already see them in that final consummation: Behold—one glorious Son comprised of many members, knit and framed together as ONE NEW MAN."

With breathless anticipation we move back to earth; how wonderful to see that which really determines and governs all ends, all goals, all destiny and intention. We shall never forget the secret we have learned: THE ULTIMATE CONCEPTION ISSUES OUT OF THE FATHER BECAUSE OF WHAT HE CHIEFLY IS IN HIS BEING AND NATURE. And we discover how every other conception must be related to THIS ULTIMATE CONCEPTION.

THE

ULTIMATE

FOUNDATION

WHY DOES A LIFE-WORK
CRASH OR COLLAPSE?

LEARNING TO RECOGNIZE
THE FOUNDATION.

ARE YOU CONTROLLED BY
THE "PARTY SPIRIT?"

IT WAS way back in 1954. Word had reached me that most of our conference grounds had burned to the ground. Now I had returned home and stood looking over what was left — mostly ashes and ruins. There remained very little of the thirteen buildings except the Chapel after the fire had swept through. Years of dreaming and planning had been swept away as in one fleeting moment; weeks and weeks of sweat and toil had gone up in empty smoke; thousands and thousands of dollars had seemingly been sacrificed for naught. I would have to admit, that as I stood there pondering, I could not help but ask: "Lord, — Why has this happened? What are You wanting to say? Don't let me miss Your lesson!" There are those times in which God can get awfully close to us — and when He can speak most loudly and emphatically. This was His time!

WHY DOES A LIFE-WORK CRASH OR COLLAPSE?

H AS HE NOT recorded in His Word, "The preparations of the heart in man . . . is from the Lord" (Proverbs 16:1)? Surely in His full knowledge God does prepare our hearts for that which is ahead. Without my realizing it, He had been doing just that! As I stood looking through bleary eyes filled with tears, no one could ever hear more comforting admonition than I heard. It was not an audible voice, but it was a most penetrating voice that communicated to me His own concern as He said: "My son — all is not lost. Rejoice that in this lesson you need not become bitter, but better; for you shall now come to understand the difference between a life work that is built on THE FOUNDATION and one which is merely built on "another foundation."

There were some things which suddenly became so clear — crystal clear. As never before I realized just how much work resulted from the vision of man's own heart, how much was wrought merely in human energies, to satisfy man's own private ambition.. For the first time I realized what THE FOUNDATION really was. I had always assumed this meant "building for Christ." Now I knew it was not *just work* done for Him, *but Him*. It was building the very life of Christ into others. Thus Christ Himself becomes in each one, in each church and in His whole Body the very Fountainhead and then the Increase.

While many are being preoccupied with great exploits for Him, they have missed this simple secret. It is not work, activity, occupation or building; it is Christ Himself — Him working.   Now then I realized what it would mean to build upon THE FOUNDATION and according to His pattern. It was not our working, but rather His working by the Spirit through us—one life touching another life and moulding it in a spiritual way. This was producing gold, silver and precious stones which are eternal and could not be destroyed by fire.

Yet here is the first essential. Only as man will know the severing work of the Cross in him, turning him from the lust to build or carve out a private kingdom in which he can glory, will God begin to share that larger vision and ultimate purpose of building only on THE FOUN-DATION and according to His pattern. I wept and rejoiced! I thanked God for His own unveiling. What I had seen I knew I could hardly really share with others, for mere words seemed too inadequate.

As I got up from my knees the Lord was adding one final reminder: "Son, you can rejoice that as a young man you have seen this crash and collapse of just a few years of labor. There are many men who have finished their whole earthly course and then see their life-work tumble when it is too late to make any changes." I could not help but thank Him again and again. How strange that the things which at first seem so bitter can be changed to the sweet. Since that day it has been my constant prayer that (1) I would always clearly recognize THE FOUNDATION which is already laid and not build upon any sandy foundations of private ambition; and (2) that I would increasingly learn how to minister by the Spirit and not in the energy of the flesh; so that in the end I may have built not wood, hay and stubble, but gold, silver and precious stones which are eternal and precious UNTO HIM.

GOD HAD BEEN PREPARING

Now in the beginning when I said that "the preparations of the heart . . . is from the Lord," I was referring to a little booklet which the Lord had previously directed to my hand. In reading this booklet, THE CRASH OR COLLAPSE OF A LIFE WORK, written by my dear friend, Paul Billheimer, God had started preparing for what was ahead. Through it He had spoken most pointedly and emphatically. It was His own way of preparing me for the crash which was soon to come. Let me share a few paragraphs from the booklet with you:

"For other foundation can no man lay than that is laid, which is Jesus Christ. *Now if any man build upon this foundation* gold, silver, precious stones, wood hay, stubble; Every man's work shall be made manifest: for the day shall declare it, because it shall be revealed by fire; . . . If any man's work abide which he hath built thereupon, he shall receive a reward. If any man's work shall be burned, he shall suffer loss: but he himself shall be saved; yet so as by fire" (1 Corinthians 3:11-15).

"These verses set forth a picture, very familiar in the Orient in Paul's day and also in ours, in which are stately palaces of marble and granite, with roof and columns glittering with gold and silver decorations, and close by these, the wretched hovels of the poor and outcast, made of wood and straw and stubble. In his mind's eye the apostle saw the flames of a great conflagration sweeping over the scene, in which all buildings of combustible material were completely consumed, while those of imperishable construction remained undamaged after the fire had exhausted itself. The apostle is warning Christian workers, by this figure, that some day their life work, done in the Name of Christ, will be subjected to the fire of Christ's judgment and that whatsoever is useless or of no permanent value will be destroyed.

"To some it may be a new (and I hope to all it may be a startling) thought, that it is possible for a Christian worker, even one who is truly born again, and maybe one who has spent his entire life in strenuous work in Christ's Name to be saved while his entire life work is destroyed. Such an one would be in the position of a man whose house has been burned; the man himself is saved, but his property, all that the man has built or accumulated in a lifetime of toil and has valued as the fruit of his labor is gone. He may not himself have suffered any bodily injury; he may have escaped from the fire himself unscathed, but he is so stripped that his whole life work has been for nothing.

"So shall it be with some Christian workers who may be even zealous and energetic, who pass into that heavenly state, hearing behind them as they enter, the crash of all they have been building up in a lifetime — leaving only a ghastly charred ruin and a cloud of dust. To have been so utterly useless to Him, to have spent their life building up a pretentious and imposing structure which at last tumbles like a house of sticks which it is, to come to the end and find that not one solid brick in the eternal building was laid by them, that none of their mistaken toil was to be accepted into the eternal—must be unspeakably sad. But such is the end that some Christian workers may be preparing for themselves. They are to enter into a life in which the nature and character of the work they have done in this world shall bring upon itself utter destruction or enduring recognition and reward. The new life they are to pass into shall absolutely annihilate what is not in keeping with it and leaven only what is useful and congruous to it.

"Surely it will be a solemn day for that Christian worker, evangelist, pastor, teacher or ecclesiastical leader who sees all these works which he so honestly believed to be for God, vanishing as worthless stubble in the searching fire of the judgment seat of Christ, which will purge away all the dross of his human doings and leave only that which is of value in God's sight. All the work that has the stamp of self-seeking upon it will then be burnt up. Gold, silver, and precious stone-work is done wholly upon God's line, for the glory of Christ alone and in which no trace of self appears.

"It might give some of us pause, if we knew that in reality, judgment is being passed and decision rendered as to the moral quality of our work even now, day by day. We are too wont to put off the day of judgment to some dim and distant future. What a difference it would tend to make in our work if we realized that we are constantly under the eye of the Judge. In Hebrews 12:23 the writer says to the believers, 'Ye are come to God the Judge of all.' It is a present thing. Day by day God is NOW weighing the value of our work in the light of eternity and rendering decision as to its ultimate worth. The results of that judgment, withheld from our eyes here, will be made manifest before all men at the judgment seat of Christ. There is much work today that looks very well in the eyes of men, that is praised very highly by church leaders, which yet may be utterly rejected by Christ in that day" (Paul Billheimer in THE CRASH OR COLLAPSE OF A LIFE WORK).

IS IT "OF MEN" OR "OF GOD"?

You can begin to see how God could prepare my heart in reading these lines. He was wanting to show me the difference between His ways and my own ways, His energy of the Spirit and my own energy of the flesh. He wanted to emphasize how all that is not originated by Him, that is not executed by His strength and energy and done alone for His glory will be consumed in the fiery test. And what is so tragic and blinding — is that I had convinced myself it *was* "for Him." Apart from "seeing things in His light" I was as one blinded. All I had originated, carried on and done for and by self, no matter how religious or successful it seemed to be, would be utterly destroyed in that day. Nothing except what God originates and executes will be revealed as having any value for eternity, and motive will be seen to be more important than accomplishment. What is done through Christ, though unpretentious, will be seen to stand the test, while that which is done for selfish or private ambition — though glorious in human eyes, will appear for what it is, only shadow and not substance: wood, hay and stubble. Since that glorious day of unveiling, the ministry has been different. I have come in an increasing way to appreciate Christ, THE FOUNDATION, and to know that God will only build upon Him, and according to Him. We shall see how *this is the message* of the journals this year.

38

A DISCERNING PASTOR COMMENTS:

When I observe the various religious efforts today, I wonder how men can continue on so blindly. One man in his ministry can gather a large congregation and build a grand monument of bricks only to have it seemingly collapse and crash in a few short years when he moves off the scene. Why? I have pondered if this is really according to God's pattern. Does anything, really built by God and unto Him collapse, or does it abide forever? Does such a builder really recognize THE FOUNDATION which is already laid, or is he guilty of carving out a little kingdom which appears to be for God, yet really is for himself?

LEARNING TO RECOGNIZE THE FOUNDATION.

WHAT does Paul mean when he insists that Jesus Christ is the Only Foundation? "For other foundation can no man lay than that is laid, which is Jesus Christ." From this verse it would seem that there are those who do attempt to lay other foundations which are really only pseudo-foundations; therefore they cannot endure. Is it possible that so much of our present day religious confusion results from building in our own

39

way and upon our own sandy foundations of private ambition? If so—one thing is surely imperative: we must clearly understand the difference between THE FOUNDATION and "other foundations."

This seemed to be the primary burden in Paul's writing to the Corinthians: to help them understand how they are laborers together with God building upon the *one foundation*, and all should be building one single superstructure.

In writing to the Corinthians the apostle is showing the tendency of certain teachers in their midst to overpress their own interpretations of the truth and so to make parties under their leadership. In warning them perhaps Paul would have pictured it (see diagram) by showing them these different foundations with the resulting different superstructures which would grow up. If they recognized THE FOUNDATION and worked as "laborers together with God" they would also understand the spiritual house which He is building, while if they were building on "another foundation," the inevitable outgrowth would be building their own visible kingdom. But notice also the hidden footing under each foundation. This pictures the motive which is hidden from view.

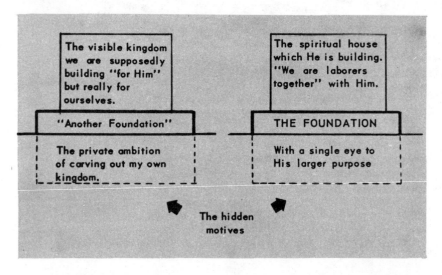

Paul would insist that once we have been truly identified with Christ in His death, we have also become identified with Him in a new motive and purpose for living. Henceforth we are not "to live unto ourselves but unto Him"—this is the new and only footing for the resurrected life. But if the work of the Cross has not touched the deepest areas of the life and ministry, men will most surely build their own kingdom upon the hidden footing of private ambition. And alas, many have convinced themselves that their ministry and motives *are* adjusted at the Cross and wholly upon the proper line and foundation.

Perhaps these most searching questions can help us test our own motives, can help us realize whether we are carving out our own kingdom, or truly living and pouring out our lives unto Him for building His spiritual house:

LET US CHECK OUR MOTIVES

Do I attempt to draw men to myself and into my orbit so as to use them for my church or little kingdom, or do I seek always to thrust them upon Christ and what He desires for their life and ministry even if they never become related to my work or vision? Without realizing what he was saying, one pastor admitted: "I never waste my time visiting in our local hospital, for almost all the patients come from nearby towns and already belong to other churches." Another pastor who came to see how self-relating his ministry had been confessed: "I'm ashamed that I have visited only my own members – how guilty I have been of seeing folk only as they related to my work."

Do I make others more dependent upon me and the spiritual food I can give them, or make them more dependent upon the Lord as their source? Do I teach them how to heed my words, or how to become alive to His speaking through His own Word? Do I secretly enjoy making others dependent upon me so it will be difficult for them to accept another teacher or spiritual leader, by winning their affections and pampering their little prejudices? In these past twenty years what a shocking time it has been for me as God broke up the little honeymoons with those who have been won or fed under our ministry. Yet – when we are unwilling to thrust them upon HIM, then He must allow some misunderstanding, some unveiling of our own frailties and blunders, some drastic crossing of purpose and vision – anything to break up the little "love affair" and release them from inordinate attachments and knowing one another after the flesh.

Do I, perhaps unwittingly, build upon my own gift and ministry so as to remain essential, or am I seeking always to build up the gift and ministry of others so I can soon be released or move out? Am I really reproducing myself in others so as to have a manifold ministry throughout the whole world, yet never to have anything visible or concrete to glory in for myself. Then all I shall have is the deep inner sense that God is getting more lives truly upon HIS FOUNDATION – those who are living wholly according to the divine pattern of ministry.

Do I rejoice when I see those "we" have won (that is, the Lord working through me) begin to fill the pews of every other group or fellowship? Do I rejoice when all our workers go out to help in other fields until it almost appears that our place has become a spawning ground for all the other fish bowls of the area? This Proverb takes on new meaning: "There is that scattereth, and yet increaseth; and there

41

is that withholdeth more than is meet, but it tendeth to poverty" (11:24). Oh, how one should rejoice when he sees the enlarging of his ministry to reach into every part of the world. But such rejoicing can only come when we have truly "seen" *the One Foundation.*

Can I rejoice when, after many years, I have nothing visible or monumental to which I can point to and glory in as the fruit of my labors, even though many of my friends around me have achieved unusual success (?) in building great kingdoms (of course they say "for the Lord") from which they can siphon off an illicit satisfaction? Have I learned the glorious lesson that real, true, lasting satisfaction only comes *from HIM* when we have not sought *it* — but *only HIM?* For then He becomes our satisfaction and we can "endure" when others feel sorry for us because we live by what they call a mistaken conception of life and ministry.

Do I insist upon the "letter-acceptance" of my private interpretations so as to bring lives into my orbit and into subjection to my ministry? If so — like almost all others — I too, have my own sign of circumcision (the separating mark) by which I can claim men as standing for *my vision,* or *belonging to my persuasion.* Look down through the centuries, and note how every fragment or faction of people building upon their own private foundations have always emphasized their mark or sign of circumcision. Nor will they really accept or wholly fellowship you until they have brought you into full submission to their peculiar mark of circumcision. Whether it be some external kind of garb, some exact mode of baptism, some verbal expression of doctrine, some exact experience or some exacting interpretation of church form — these all have become the gathering point or foundation upon which one must stand before he is truly loyal or accepted into full fellowship. How subtle and how divisive is the enemy in turning men to "other foundations" so as to keep them from enjoying Him and the common expression of His life and fellowship.

In taking this little test of our motives and methods — we trust that the Holy Spirit will make clear what it means to recognize THE FOUNDATION which is already laid, and how we are called to build according to His pattern.

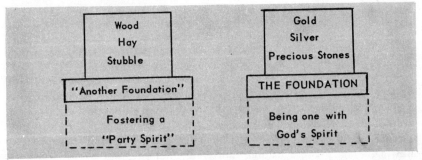

Wood Hay Stubble	Gold Silver Precious Stones
"Another Foundation"	THE FOUNDATION
Fostering a "Party Spirit"	Being one with God's Spirit

WE SAT in a circle as a group of fellow workers sharing as the Lord would direct. For some time the fellowship and spirit was sweet and there was no confusion. Then it became very manifest that one who was yet building *his own kingdom* and promoting his own program was becoming defensive and closed. It was as though he were fearful of certain conclusions which might be forced upon him. To most of us it became obvious that if he were truly teachable, perhaps the Holy Spirit would unveil some method or motive in him that was wrong and it would eventuate in readjustment, or even in needing to discontinue his little kingdom building. For all of us — without any words or instruction to that effect — it became crystal clear whether we were open or protective, whether we were striving or calm in spirit and gentle in attitude, whether we were partial and divisive or easy to be entreated.

It was as though by One Spirit we were being taught — and were freely drinking of that One Spirit. Someone has well said that, "in real intimate fellowship with anyone, we are sure to drink of their spirit or the fellowship will cease." Surely we must know when to be "closed to the spirit of another" but we must also learn, how to be continually open to THE HOLY SPIRIT.

ARE YOU CONTROLLED BY THE "PARTY SPIRIT" ?

IN THE Corinthian letter Paul seems to show clearly how men are either *one with God's Spirit* or they are for selfish reasons *fostering a party spirit.* It becomes obvious that whichever foundation one stands upon determines which spirit he drinks of and is governed by, and determines how he will build. The apostle would remind us that all religious work which is built up by the use of party spirit will in *that day* — if not sooner — be consumed as mere wood, hay and stubble.

Today how many religious institutions rest upon "another foundation." They have been built up by emphasizing some nonessential as the basis of fellowship, drawing others into their orbit by cutting them off from fellowship with other believers thus making a schism in the Body of Christ. "It is altogether possible that the truth in Christ is so varied and many sided that no one man or body of people can present it in its full orbed symmetry" (P.E.B.). I can very well understand that God might awaken one man or body of people especially to recover some phase of truth which has been neglected, but for them to continually emphasize that phase as though it were *all* that really mattered, is to insure division and lopsidedness. The tendency to substitute that *one phase* as though it were the whole, to make fellowship rest in a common opinion rather than in a common life, is to set up an idol, to substitute another god for Christ, to begin "another foundation" instead of recognizing THE FOUNDATION.

How easy it is for those who have never experienced identification at the Cross to foster a party spirit and to use it as an instrument by which to build a work which must some day perish in the flames. What is a "party spirit"? It is that which causes men to be more zealous for their own view, for their own vision, for their own methods and their own group than for Christ and the eternal purpose of God.

Let us beware of becoming movement minded! Live *unto* and *for* the whole Body of Christ or we will find ourselves stranded upon *another foundation*. With simplicity of heart, belong to Christ rather than to any man or any emphasis of truth. We may rightly appreciate and give due honor to the individual or church which was the instrument of our salvation and growth in grace, but when our love for our church breaks or hinders our fellowship with God's true people in any other group, it has gotten in the wrong place — it is to that degree interfering with our fellowship with Christ. God says of His people, "Whosoever toucheth you toucheth the apple of mine eye." When we refuse to fellowship one with whom Christ is in fellowship, we are — in a sense — limiting our full measure of fellowship with Christ.

It is important to remember that we can fellowship individuals as those who share the life of Christ even though we may not find basis for fellowship with (or partake of) the system or *other foundation* in which they are yoked. (We shall consider the foundation of fellowship in another chapter).

THE FOUNDATION OF THE PARTY SPIRIT

The root or foundation of the party spirit is always self interest. Any effort to separate a believer or a group of believers from another and draw them into the orbit of my personal leadership or into the orbit of my group is almost always motivated by plain unvarnished private ambition. It is done often with the purpose of enlarging my prestige, ecclesiastical or financial reward. It is sometimes the result of spiritual pride, for it flatters our vanity to bring others to bow down to our theological idols and come under the spell of our leadership.

Consider the cost! It is well known that a man can expect no recognition of any kind in many tightly formed groups unless he shows loyalty to that group even at the cost of the highest principles. And some men yield that kind of loyalty because they know they will be penalized ecclesiastically if they do not. Thus a great organization is built up and maintained by means of the party spirit. There will certainly be a vast conflagration at the Judgment Seat of Christ, for all religious work which is carried on with a view of self-advantage and private ambition will go up in flames.

The question is raised: How can you build up and hold together a work in a world of so much competition, proselytizing and so many unfair methods, if you do not have something human by which to hold it together? Our answer is this: "All that is held together by anything else than *His Spirit* or built upon any other than *His foundation* will fall apart and go to pieces in *that day* if not before; therefore it is not worth the effort now.

Consider the narrowing effect of the party spirit. The Corinthians were each dividing into little factions, following men and manifesting the "I'm right spirit." Some emphasized Paul, for they loved teaching and the intellectual diet. Another group gathered around Apollos, for no doubt his oratory and fluency of words stirred them to action. Still another group followed Peter, for his seemingly practical ministry and understanding was more in sympathy with their ups and downs. But there was yet a fourth group who insisted the others were divisive in their interpretations. These proudly insisted: "We are of Christ — you are wrong — we are the only ones who are right, for we follow only Christ."

Let us admit, that perhaps in principle and doctrine, these who were *of Christ* seemed to be *more* right. Yet they were wrong. They fostered a party spirit, in that they were using Christ for their own advantage and strange as it may seem, were building their work on *another foundation.* Their wrong "I'm right spirit" was proof enough that they were building upon a wrong foundation, that they were not wholly settled *upon* and living *unto* the Lord Jesus. When we have truly learned to labor and build with Him, we enjoy watching how the Holy Spirit works. He does not allow us to vindicate ourselves nor establish our own positions. When He takes over we do not need to foster the party or "I'm right spirit."

Here was Paul's answer to their party spirit. What narrowness! What foolishness, cutting themselves off from all the others. What foolish acting as babes. How could they glory in mere men? Did they not know that "all things" were theirs and that they all needed the ministry and help of Paul, of Apollos, and of Peter?

Even so it comes down to our day — the same party spirit cuts us off from the larger ministry of God's servants to His Body. Is not Luther ours, and Calvin too, also Wesley and Whitefield as well as Finney and even the pastor down the street in another church? Yes, Paul insists that when we have truly recognized THE FOUNDATION we are able to appreciate and receive every ministry which He has given. We shall live in One Spirit and drink freely from all the wisdom and knowledge that God shares in building His Spiritual House.

The lines are becoming more clearly drawn between that which is "of men" and that which is "of God." The hour is fast approaching when there will be an increased shaking of everything that can be shaken, "... that those things which cannot be shaken may remain. Wherefore we receiving a kingdom which cannot be moved, let us have grace, whereby we may serve God acceptably with reverence and godly fear" (Hebrews 12:27, 28).

Therefore we can expect the testing of our motives. Work that is done with a view to some selfish advantage, advancement, better salary, greater ecclesiastical influence and recognition, social popularity and worldly success is really all of a piece with secular work and one laboring with these motives had better get into secular work altogether. The use of religion, the employment of sacred things to build a secular and private kingdom will surely end in sore judgment. It is true that God has His place for each one to work, and when He is honored as Head He will help them build according to pattern.

"But there is one thing that is primary with God: that is the exaltation and glorification of His Son. He will not be a part to glorifying any individual, any group movement, any body of people or ecclesiastical system apart from Christ. All that God has ordained, all ministries, all gifts, all appointments, all positions, all relationships — all exist solely for THE INCREASE OF CHRIST. No one in a God established order has any position or ministry which is merely official. In the order which God sanctions, there is no ministration of any kind which is given for any other purpose than THE INCREASE OF CHRIST. When any other thing, the lifting up of any other leader, the advantage of any man or set of men comes into the motive, then God is not interested" (P.E.B.).

Finally we are all faced with these questions? What is the hidden motive which governs our life and service? Upon what foundation are we building? What spirit controls us? Are we building wood, hay and stubble, or gold, silver and precious stones? There is no in-between. We are either on THE FOUNDATION or seeking to build "other foundations."   ★★

IS YOUR APPROACH RIGHT? In observing how a wise counselor dealt with a Jehovah's Witness one day, I learned the following valuable lessons. In fact here are principles we should use in helping any person. (1) Having first established a real sense of confidence and genuine concern for truth, then suggest that together you might consider some of the foundations of his and your beliefs.

As the conversation proceeded that day, I remembered how often I had heard folk disagree over some of the most insignificant details which really were quite *beside the point*. So I learned (2) how important it is to know, so as to help the other to know that some issues are basic and that others naturally follow out of those.

Here I was observing a counselor, trained by God, who had learned and was practicing Paul's exhortation: "In meekness instructing those that oppose themselves...," (3) I also learned—as it was demonstrated before my eyes—that most men, even without realizing it, are holding convictions which can be clearly shown to be contrary to moral principles or even to their own good judgment. Men do oppose themselves and not know it until shown. Before two hours had passed, I saw the real wisdom in always heading for the basic premise (or foundation stones) upon which a person's experience or theology is built. I was thus convinced (and convicted in myself) that the Holy Spirit eagerly waits for intelligent servants willing to cooperate with God's ways.

LEARNING HOW TO PULL OUT THE RUG!

THERE ARE a great many followers of these cult groups—the Mormons, Christian Scientists and Jehovah's Witnesses—who, like many sincere church members do not bother to think clearly regarding *their foundation*. Therefore they do not understand nor really have any "theological rug" which can be "pulled out." With such cases it is well to suggest that with paper and pencil you might draw the various levels of each building and show how each has a foundation which is completely different. To courteously and in meekness show fairly what they believe and what you believe will quite manifestly demonstrate the evident weakness and strength of each foundation. You need to remember and remind them that even with a perfect house, if the foundation fails — the house falls.

Why should we waste our time with mere incidentals? Who cares about the color, the size windows, the number of rooms, the shape or the location of the house if the foundation will not support it?

So with a Jehovah's Witness it is foolish to argue about hell and its purpose or duration, about the chosen 144,000, about the invisible coming of Christ in 1914 to set up His earthly kingdom before He makes Himself visible to our eyes, or about whether one should pray in public or only in his closet. I must admit how often I used to get drawn into some of these side issues before I knew a better approach. There are a hundred, perhaps a thousand incidental issues one must avoid. To prove or disprove any or all of these would still leave each one yet confirmed in his previous convictions. You see every one of us has a *controlling conception*. We must understand and deal with that!

In the beginning of his many-volume studies, Dr. C. T. Russell, the early father of the Jehovah's Witnesses (don't be confused by their continual change of name), sets forth his primary viewpoint and helps us to understand the foundation upon which all his theology is built. It goes something like this:

> God has set a bountiful table of blessings and good
> things for the whole human race to enjoy.

Before many sentences have been written you become very much aware of one thing. Man is to be the great benefactor, the primary recipient, and *the glorious center* around which and for which all things exist. To this end God has dedicated Himself in establishing a universal kingdom so that man might truly reap all these benefits. Therefore God becomes the Great Servant of man.

To the majority, without any spiritual perception, perhaps this sounds wonderful: that the eternal God has dedicated Himself to man's welfare and is now making all His plans that man might enjoy a great feast of good things. How can selfish man refuse this invitation to sit at such a table?

Having drawn two foundations (A) on the paper you write in them: "man is central" and "God is central." Then you ask, "What is selfish man's first and greatest need? According to your group and several others which we might name, man needs a strong, righteous government to establish and enforce peace throughout the world. Without this promised kingdom or government you are sure we cannot enjoy the glorious millenial reign. So it is imperative, both you and I believe, that Jesus Christ return to establish His kingdom." (With this the majority can hardly help but agree.)

Then you ask: "But have you ever seen any force, any law or government which was powerful enough to hinder selfish man from getting his own way? Of course history proves there has been none. Even when

48

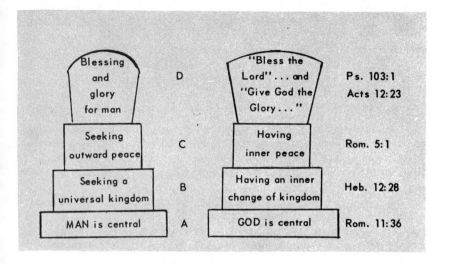

Blessing and glory for man	D	"Bless the Lord"... and "Give God the Glory..."	Ps. 103:1 / Acts 12:23
Seeking outward peace	C	Having inner peace	Rom. 5:1
Seeking a universal kingdom	B	Having an inner change of kingdom	Heb. 12:28
MAN is central	A	GOD is central	Rom. 11:36

Jesus Christ does come to set up His outward kingdom you see it will have necessitated something else first. It is all too evident that none of man's attempt at enforcement has ever been adequate to meet man's first problem. Man's greatest need is a change of heart. That means Christ sitting on the inner throne: the heart.

Now as you draw (B) the next two levels on each foundation, you show how his group teaches that man should seek an outward righteous kingdom thus bringing about peace, but that you believe man first needs to have an inner change of government in his own heart—thus giving him inner peace.

Then in drawing the next level (C) you show another important difference: how some are seeking outward peace while others having not sought peace, have received inner peace through Christ living in their heart.

Finally you show how there are two completely different purposes expressed in every life as you draw the top circle (D). One group lives to *receive* blessing and glory for man, while the other group lives to follow the Bible exhortation to "Bless the Lord" and "Give God the glory."

How different are these two houses built on opposite foundations. They are like the two men Jesus pictured in Matthew 7:24-28. The man who built his house upon the sand lost all, while the one who built upon THE ROCK (God) withstood the storms. There is something strange and wonderful about the faithfulness of the Holy Spirit to unveil and convict man of his selfishness and wanting to use God for his own ends. Again it is absolutely essential that we recognize how different is the ministry and approach of the Jehovah's Witness. They always emphasize a *national message*, while as fundamentalist we usually emphasize the *personal message*. Men who do not understand this difference can hardly appreciate the total disregard which the Jehovah's Witnesses have for "being born again." Being, above all, kingdom conscious, they see the restoration of "spiritual Israel" as the only great means of peace and righteousness. But they ignore the spiritual birth which makes such possible. For this reason they now build kingdom halls everywhere to instruct and cooperate with the now-present though invisible Lord to establish His kingdom here on earth.

Surely as the Holy Spirit sends a shaft deep into the empty aching heart, one can almost always expect a reply like this: "Oh, I never saw it this way before. But—the way you talk and show the proper foundation doesn't seem to be the way of most churches and members I have met. You are different."

You may then want to tell them it is because the Lord has not only changed your *inner government* but has also given you a *proper viewpoint* in relating all things to God. You will admit that perhaps too many people and churches he has encountered are blindly building on the same sandy foundation as he, and for that very reason they have not been able to help the Jehovah's Witnesses—or anyone else—out of a self-centered viewpoint and life of selfish grasping. You might even question him: "Perhaps that is the real reason your aching heart left the (whatever connection you previously had) to study the teaching of Jehovah's Witness?"

It is important to show how every foundation has its hidden footing, which is really the motive of the heart. As long as *man is central*, his unregenerate heart will continue a "selfish grasping." But when man becomes a new creature in Christ Jesus, a *new King* has come to the throne and shed His love abroad in the heart so that he is then controlled by a "love that gives." These are the hidden motives which determine the purpose of life.

As I indicated earlier in the opening, that day I learned to trust the Holy Spirit to unveil motives that are wrong. When the foundation is clearly shown to be wrong the heart will be pricked, even though the head may plead "confusion." One who is honest will usually begin to admit some of his own skepticism and questionings. A discerning eye can see that a building is about to topple.

As we lifted our heads from praying that God would give continued unveiling of His truth to our hearts, I saw an openness, an honesty and a willingness to be taught—it was remarkable! It was of God. Wisdom knew better than to rush for an immediate outward decision. Surely one was already being made in the inner man. There was a new light in the eyes. God was ploughing deep.

Then my friend—the counselor—turning to me asked: "What would happen to that little table with the lamp on it, if suddenly I pulled that rug out from under it?" I knew exactly what he meant, for that afternoon I also had been LEARNING HOW TO PULL OUT THE RUG!

THE

ULTIMATE
MINISTRY

A MINISTRY OF APPARENT
SUCCESS—OR INCREASE

PREACHING ABOUT THE CROSS, OR
THE PREACHING OF THE CROSS

IN OUR MINISTRY . . . .
WHAT ARE WE OCCUPIED WITH?

TO PARTICIPATE IN
THIS ULTIMATE MINISTRY

FOR ABOUT 15 years we have observed a church as it has passed through two kinds of ministry and emphasis:

The first pastor in his ministry enjoyed an unusual spiritual increase. Though at times it seemed his preaching and practice of the Cross would turn everyone away, yet God was faithful to give His own increase. Indeed there were new kernels of corn being "born" and then planted around about— a continual process. Out from this church flowed individual ministries and gospel teams to share His Life and reality. Almost every church, home and street corner felt the impact of this outreach. It seemed this was a church bent on ministering to every part of Christ's Body in that area. With such a broadside scattering of lives, one often wondered if there would be anyone left in church for the pastor to minister to. Strangely! But as more left, there were many more to take their places. In their liberality of giving to the whole Body of Christ, the Lord graciously gave HIS OWN INCREASE.

The second pastor came to this church and another kind of ministry and emphasis followed. It was not immediately perceptible, but gradually this pastor's conception became evident and his intentions were made known. Instead of encouraging folk to move out in a ministry, he insisted that they should be "in their place, working in their own church—faithful every Sunday." He impressed upon them the need to build their church, not every other church in the valley. It seemed so right—so logical. Indeed the folk needed to be taught and better established before they went out! Surely they needed to build a strong local center as an example that other churches might follow. Perhaps without realizing it, the emphasis changed from "bringing hearts to the Lord" to "bringing them to their church."

Now, after seven or eight years of this emphasis the church has every appearance of success, yet underneath there is a deep sense of spiritual poverty—emptiness, unreality. There is little flow of life! The church is moving on the momentum started in the past. In living unto itself, it has become much like a bin of grain—grain which should have been planted long ago. All we have pictured would emphasize clearly that there are two kinds of ministry:

A MINISTRY OF APPARENT SUCCESS OR
A MINISTRY OF DIVINE INCREASE

SOONER OR LATER every individual will be faced in his ministry with *living for his own part* or *living for God's whole.* Here we touch the hidden motive which governs our ministry. With a Sunday school teacher it may be building just his own class or integrating them into the whole life of the church; with a pastor it may be building his own congregation or building the whole Body of Christ in that locality; with a district leader it may be building his own region instead of living unto the whole; even in the home one member may live unto himself and by his individualism hinder the whole family. While our motive may not be discernible, our kind of ministry will always "give us away." Again we picture two different foundations for building two kinds of ministry: There is one which (with) holdeth and one which scattereth. If the reader requires a clear—cut principle to stand upon, consider these verses in Proverbs 11:24-31.

> "There is that scattereth, and yet increaseth;
> and there is that withholdeth more than is meet,
> but it tendeth to poverty (vs 24).
> The liberal soul shall be made fat: and he that
> watereth shall be watered also himself" (vs 25).

What a paradox this seems! Yet with a discerning eye one can see this demonstrated, not only in the church mentioned above, but in many churches across the land. Let no one misunderstand that we rejoice in the great increase in attendance in any church, but we must not be fooled into accepting such as the guarantee of spiritual increase. Nor should we assume that this modern impetus in building new church sanctuaries demonstrates THE INCREASE OF GOD.

One day the prophet Hosea looked out upon the apparent success and increase of Israel. But with his discerning eye he could distinguish that their seeming increase was actually spiritual poverty. Listen to his warning:

"Israel is an empty vine, he bringeth forth fruit unto himself . . ." (Hosea 10:1-2). Is not this God's controversy with the modern church of today? As we háve pictured (in the diagram), there is great building of our own little kingdoms. In living for our own part we are forced to

TWO MINISTRIES WHICH OFTEN APPEAR ALIKE:

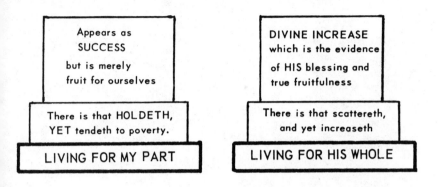

Appears as
SUCCESS

but is merely
fruit for ourselves

There is that HOLDETH,
YET tendeth to poverty.

LIVING FOR MY PART

DIVINE INCREASE
which is the evidence
of HIS blessing and
true fruitfulness

There is that scattereth,
and yet increaseth

LIVING FOR HIS WHOLE

"hold". This is according to our hidden motive: "fruit unto ourselves" Notice also that Hosea speaks of a time in the history of Israel when "according to the multitude of his fruit (Israel's not God's) he hath increased the altars; according to the goodness of his land they have made goodly images." Israel was building places of worship in every suitable hill or forest —but (like images)—it merely brought glory and satisfaction to their own heart—not to God.

Finally in verse two we have God uncovering the real motive in their ministry: "Their heart is divided..." As it was with Israel, so it is with us. Our heart will be secretly carving out some little part of the vineyard as a way to demonstrate our own success—we are eager for the fruit for ourselves. But when we have been adjusted at the Cross, our ministry will be dedicated unto God's whole purpose; we shall be content to scatter and plant for we know that in due season, God will give the divine increase which will manifest true fruitfulness unto Himself.

I suppose there is some reader, like myself, who has observed such extreme liberality in giving away that when it came time for planting there was nothing left to plant—and hence could be no harvest in the fall. For the majority who tend toward selfishness there is a little phrase, which is quite important. Consider how in Proverbs 11:24 God does encourage us to use wisdom in our liberality. "There is that withholdeth *more than is meet...*" In this phrase: *more than is meet* we have God's instruction to keep sufficient grain for planting, or in the case of a church to keep sufficient workers to properly conduct the ministry of the church. In our dedication to follow certain principles, God never allows the extremes which unsanctified judgment pursues.

THROUGHOUT THE WEEK as we visited in many of the homes of the church-people, certain desperate situations became apparent to me. I found myself selecting illustrations and designing messages calculated to expose these problems and to effect the cure. However, by the end of the week it was obvious I was only preaching at the people; the Holy Spirit was not sharpening the truth or applying it. Indeed I had shared truth with excellent application. But herein was the trouble: *I was doing it* and it therefore brought no response.

In desperation I determined to spend the night in prayer, asking God for a breaking among the people. God heard! But His way was to start a breaking in me which unveiled why mine was . . . . .

A MINISTRY OF DEATH
INSTEAD OF LIFE.

GOD'S WAY with me is often so graphic. After hours of waiting to understand why my preaching did not break the people or convict them, I was reminded of Elijah and how he had recovered the axe head for the students. Then it began to unfold—yes, that was exactly my problem. I felt like a woodman chopping at the trees, but the axe head had fallen from the handle. I saw how I had only been whipping the people with the handle. When there is no cutting power it is because the head is gone.

Surely this was the secret! Without the anointing of the Holy Spirit there could be no sharpness or cutting. Indeed the sharpened axe head is to the woodman as the anointing is to the servant of the Lord. Only one who has known the importance of a sharp edge could realize his helplessness without it.

Then I realized this was only the beginning of what God was to show me. The further question was, how to keep the Holy Spirit's anointing continually in the ministry. As I pondered about the axe, I recalled how a friend had questioned me about the three parts of an axe. I knew about the handle and the head, but had forgotten completely about the little wedge which keeps the head in place.

Then like a shaft of light exposing the darkness I saw a reality which was to change my walk as nothing else had ever changed it. I saw that one cannot rest upon a past submission. God intends for us to enjoy a daily walk in intimate fellowship. And such fellowship requires not only a crisis, but a daily practice (and a spirit) of submission. Indeed here was the important key to the secret of an anointed ministry. Submission or obedience as a daily routine was the little wedge which keeps the axe-head in place. I realized in a new way why Peter had insisted that a daily flowing of the Holy Spirit is given to them who obey (Acts 5:32). How guilty I had been of resting on the past. There had been many a crisis of submission, but God wanted a daily reality, not a past testimony. I saw that God's way to condition a life in the spirit of submission was to precipitate new issues every day so as to uncover pride, hidden reversions to the self-life, or subtle dependencies upon the soul-life. How blessed to expect and enjoy that pathway of submission which continually crosses up the old, so there may be a flowing in of His NEW LIFE.

That night I realized anew that I was demanding something of the people which I was not giving to God. I was simply asking submission—and that was what God was asking of me. The circumstance was different, but the issue was the same: submission. Is it not strange how we can know certain principles, and yet—if we do not live in that intimate fellowship of light they will slip from our attention? I had often spoken from the following verse, but now its meaning flooded with new significance.

" ... Being in readiness to punish every (insubordinate for
his) disobedience, when your own submission and obedience are fully secured and complete" (A.N.T. 2 Cor. 10:6).

How appropriate this verse was to my need. I saw how the spirit of blindness and deception could legally hold sway over these lives. I could expect no invasion by the Holy Spirit to cast down false reasonings or proud and lofty things that set themselves against God until my obedience was fulfilled. I saw more clearly than I had ever seen that this is not a battle in which our weapons are mere sermons, illustrations or clever devices for uncovering wrong, but the Holy Spirit's sharp edge is our only weapon for the overthrow and destruction of strongholds (2 Cor. 10:5).Thus we are the first stronghold that must be under full submission.

NOW NO LONGER DEATH—BUT LIFE

Immediately my ministry changed. When in brokenness I faced my own lethargy and carelessness—my own lack of instant obedience and sub-mission—then the Holy Spirit was faithful to uncover the people. Instead of whipping with an axe-handle, there was a sweet flowing of Life—His Life that no one could resist. Where there is this flowing of Life, all the letter and legality, all striving and death are set aside for the work of the Spirit.

I remembered one Fall when it was time to gather the oak leaves in our yard. I waited and waited but many of them would not fall. I would have used a pole to strip the leaves if the trees had not been so tall. But when the Spring came I discovered how wonderful is God's lesson of life. Just a few days after the sap began to flow up into the branches all those dead leaves were released. How graphically He pictured to me that my ministry had so often been a pole ministry: that is, taking a long pole and from the pulpit trying to knock off the dead things in the lives of people. Often I could not reach them—my pole was too short. And more often when I had severed some of the dead things—there they sat, stripped—but lifeless, purged—but empty of any fruit or growth. Indeed God's way is to use His Life to overcome the ravages of death. THIS IS THE MINISTRY WE NEED.

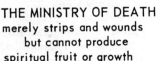

THE MINISTRY OF DEATH	THE MINISTRY OF LIFE
merely strips and wounds but cannot produce spiritual fruit or growth	automatically prunes and releases all that is excess or unnecessary.

Rom. 8:3
"...for what the law could not do...."

Rom. 8:11
"If the Spirit... in you... shall quicken...."

2 Cor. 3:6
"...the letter killeth"...but.."the Spirit giveth LIFE."

Gal. 3:5
by "the works of the law".. or.."by the hearing of faith."

A BOY WAS ONCE seen walking home after the martyr fires had been burning brightly at Smithfield. Someone said to him: "My boy, why were you there?" Like a true follower of the Lamb he replied. "I want to learn the way."

When Bloody Mary, as she has been called, had forbidden the proclamation of the simple gospel, Lawrence Sanders was constrained to obey God rather than man. When sentenced to death before the Lord Chancellor, Sanders answered: "Welcome be it, whatever the will of God shall be, either life or death; I tell you truly I have *learned* to die." Taking the stake to which he was to be chained and burned, he kissed it saying. "Welcome the Cross of Christ, welcome everlasting life."

Do such martyr stories seem to belong to another world, "to another order of life?" Shame on us that we think so! If, however, it is our eternal passion to press on to know Christ, we shall soon discover that the crucified Lord must have crucified followers; that as we glory in the Cross for our salvation, so we must embrace the Cross for crucifixion. We cannot sever the outward from the inward cross. Shame on me if I think there is a Cross for Jesus, but none for me. Let me embrace the way of the Cross and learn to die.

By L. E. Maxwell in BORN CRUCIFIED.

THE PREACHING ABOUT THE CROSS, OR

THE PREACHING OF THE CROSS

IT IS ALARMING that many evangelicals in their ministry have considered the Cross as their theme, yet they have not known it as an inward regulating power. As we have pictured (below) there is a very real difference between a *preaching about the Cross* and a *preaching of the Cross*. To fondly look away to Calvary's rugged hill and glory in the Cross is simply to know an outward Cross; to embrace the Cross inwardly and experience its changing power is to have not merely an instrumental— but an expressive ministry.

Among others there is at least one verse (1 Cor. 1:18) in which Paul explains how the Cross had become a regulating force in his life and ministry. But we shall miss the full meaning of this verse unless we discover the meaning of one word—a word which becomes a key to open the meaning which has too long been hidden. The King James version reads:

"The preaching of the cross is to them that perish foolishness, but unto us which are saved it is the power of God" (1 Cor. 1:18).

Now the term *preaching* used here is "logos" in the Greek. To leave the impression that this term implies merely a vocal declaration—as we usually consider preaching—is to miss the real issue. Surely God has something much deeper in mind than a mere *preaching about the Cross.*

We rejoice that several new translations are using: "the word (logos) of the Cross", so as to indicate that it is the expression, the divine reason or unveiling of the Cross which is vitally important. Here is the essential difference. As long as the Cross is but a proclamation it is merely a *ministry of the lip;* but when the Cross becomes incarnate as an operating principle it produces a *ministry of life.* So we can see there is a declaration (preaching) *about* the Cross, but there must also be an expression (preaching) *of* the Cross.

From eternity the Cross has been an inward regulating principle in God. Everything God does is sacrificial: i.e. giving, sharing and pouring forth from Himself. We can see the Cross in the heart of God regulating all He does. So, when the Eternal Son stepped forth from the bosom of the Father to enter this world, it was indeed the Logos of God coming forth: He was the Divine Expression.

Expression or Proclamation

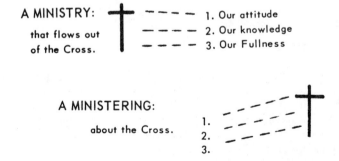

A MINISTRY:
that flows out
of the Cross.

1. Our attitude
2. Our knowledge
3. Our Fullness

A MINISTERING:
about the Cross.

1.
2.
3.

How can you express yourself if there are no adequate words? Well, the Heavenly Father had an Adequate Word. He sent forth His Son to be the very expression of Himself. And when we behold THE SON we see not merely God's Person expressed, but we can look into the very nature of God and see the inward principle of the Cross in operation. All through His earthly life we see our Lord Jesus continually giving Himself—and finally even unto the death of the Cross. So there is both the Logos of the Father—the expressing of His Person, and also the logos of the Cross—the expressing of His inward sacrificial nature.

Since every believer is to have a ministry, the question is—what do we express? We are concerned that the vast majority of ministering is merely a declaration about the Cross, but God intends for us to be expressive of the Cross.

1 THE INWARD CROSS REGULATES OUR ATTITUDE. When Mrs. Brown came home from the Sunday service her first remark was: "I don't know why I go back to that church, I never seem to get a thing out of that service." It is not beyond possibility that the church service was lacking in reality and a flowing of life, but it is most evident that she needs a rectifying in her conception of ministry. She clearly emphasized that she "went to get." There are multitudes who sit in church every Sunday whose sole pre-occupation is to be ministered unto. They sing about the Cross, talk about the Cross and preach about it—but have missed its radical working within. In God's intention we are not invited to a worship service as mere spectators—but as participators. When we have been dealt with inwardly, the Cross will help us to go to any service to minister, not merely be ministered unto.

In my observing certain lives, it has been amazing to see how some individuals can come into a service with life, light and reality exuding from their face. They can lift any service, warm any atmosphere, encourage any speaker by their receptivity. Divine Life is flowing out of their being. Such individuals have surely experienced an inward regulating of the Cross. They are always expressive—pouring forth, giving of themselves—ministering to the hearts and spirits of others. Nor do they need a pulpit for such a ministry. They overflow while in the pew, in the car, on the street or in the home. They have moved beyond a mere declaration of that redemptive work of Christ which is available to all; now they are like an open channel ministering His Life to all.

2 THE INWARD CROSS REGULATES OUR KNOWLEDGE. Who has not, at some time, reached a point when spiritual things seem stale, when preaching has lost its edge, when praying has become monotony, when reading and studying the Word has become empty and meaningless? Few will ever honestly admit such a state of unreality, even to themselves—yet it does exist. There is a reason.

If you will pardon my rather crude illustration, I like to describe it like this. We have a faucet at our kitchen sink which has several seives that mix air into the outflowing of the water. It comes out aireated—full of life, bubbling—sparkling. I think this is much like our ministry. When we share knowledge which has not passed through the seive—i.e. the Cross has not made it operative in our life—it is just a flow without life, sparkle or reality. Some people share knowledge—but there has been no regulating by the Cross—and the outflow is dead, rational and stimulating only to the mind. Other people share their experiences—but there has been no regulating by the Cross—and the outflow is empty, meaningless, almost repulsive for it is related to them and their blessing. Their experience is intended to stimulate the emotions of others, but oh the lack of reality.

I know a pastor who has taken one church after another in the past twenty years. He is a thorough, deliberate teacher of the Word who glories in getting every jot and tittle in its precise pigeon-hole. The tragedy is, that after two or three years of this ministry of knowledge, his congregation dwindles, his people get puffed up in their superior ability to interpret according to the fundamental yardstick. The outflow of knowledge has never been aireated (regulated) at the Cross—where it becomes reality—i.e. life-giving and lifting.

3 THE INWARD CROSS REGULATES OUR FULLNESS: In these days when home Bible study groups are springing up everywhere, and other groups are seeking to move into the proper New Testament order for Church ministry, this inner regulation at the Cross is becoming more necessary. It is true, at the beginning, any change in style of service will inspire or enthuse participation. Yet for an effective ministry—there must be a flow of life. We have already said there must be an adjusted attitude: coming to minister instead of being ministered unto. But when everyone comes to the service to share "out of the top of his head," the problem only deepens. One who is inclined to be intellectual will share knowledge while the others groan in boredom. Another will share his self-relating experiences which are meaningless to others.

As we look around us, we cannot fail to observe a tragic lack of spiritual reality. There is nothing about these lives to indicate fullness or overflow. They hardly have sufficient for their own needs, much less something to spare for others in the meeting.

The danger in this open sharing which is intended to allow a body—ministry is that so few come prepared—or overflowing. This does not mean that one prepares himself to share in a service by picking up some good book, or even turning to the Bible for some hastily acquired bit of knowledge. There are some types of personality whose vivacity and personal inspirition can pawn off second-hand experiences with a marked degree of (seeming) reality. But the majority cannot! There is always an undertone of unreality to the discerning ear. When things do not flow through the Cross, as a seive, there will be no regulating of experience or knowledge into fulness of reality.

Why are so many poor in reality? It is because they do not know the discipline of the Spirit. They have by-passed the Cross and its working in them. The Palmist explained it: "in pressure thou hast enlarged me" (Psalm 4:1 Darby TR). So the object of all pressure is enlargement—a bringing us to larger capacity that we may have ample to share with others when we enter the meeting. We must learn to count upon His twofold work: first of revealing to us the nature and the dimensions of reality, and secondly of bringing us into every whit of the reality He has revealed. Thus it is not a question of our capacity, or of our ability, but of the absolute faithfulness of the Holy Spirit to produce an outflow and release through our life.

Let us not despair! If we know we have embraced the inward Cross for an effective ministry, we can be sure He is faithful to accomplish that inward regulating of attitude, reality and fullness.

" Our reliance is too much ON THE CHARMS OF THIS WORLD, in drawing souls to the Gospel and to the Saviour. The Holy Spirit will not tolerate our idols. If we WILL have artistic and secular types of music, substituting unsanctified art for simple praise; if we WILL have elaborate ritual in place of simple, believing prayer; if we WILL have eloquent lectures in place of simple, earnest Gospel preaching, we must not wonder if no Shekinah fires burn in our sanctuaries."

A. T. Pierson.

WE HAD JUST BEEN SEATED in his study. There was a moment of strained silence and finally he said, "I invited you over to help me — I'm seemingly at the end of my rope. I must honestly face it. Something is wrong in my life and therefore in my ministry."

I was not surprised, though I'm sure these words would have come as a great shock to scores of ministerial friends who, I'm sure, secretly envied his prestige, apparent success and popularity. I looked around at the scores of shelves holding hundreds of carefully chosen volumes — books — all that any pastor could want in his study. I glanced at his files which I knew contained more than 20 years of extraordinary sermons — sound, scriptural, enlightening — so all his listeners would have insisted.

Why — why was this man admitting such failure? No, I repeat, it was no surprise. For in more than 15 years of traveling across this country I have heard this inner-spirit-groan from dozens of others —men whom one could hardly imagine felt that way; names I would not share with you for any reason, for I hold their trust and confidence too sacred.

Here was a dear servant of God who had tried the modern-day methods of evangelism, but was not fully cognizant of what kind of members it had added to his congregation. Here was one who had filled his pews morning and evening with an enviable attendance record, yet who inwardly had become convinced that he was merely appealing to man's soul-appetite while starving his spirit-appetite for God.

When a man opens the door and pulls aside the veneer from his own life it is time to accept his invitation. But any forced entrance, I have learned, will only create strain and resentment for it is like ploughing and planting before season. God always has HIS time — He is always working at both ends: in preparing the seed-bed and in preparing HIS seed.

So I asked him if he would like for me to share

one of the most precious secrets which the Lord
had disclosed to me more than 15 years before—
one which had utterly transformed my whole conception and purpose in the ministry. (These same
principles were then written in our book, *Come
Hither*, now out of print.)

He was interested so I asked him to turn with
me to Ezekiel 44' where I began to distinguish
between two different kinds of ministry as set
forth there.

MINISTRY—to the house or to the Lord.

I suggested that we might read together from a
small pamphlet written by Watchman Nee. I had
just found in his writings how God had disclosed
this same secret to this dear Chinese servant.
Also in reading thus it would seem more impersonal and less direct, thereby making it possible
for the Holy Spirit to make His own application to
this pastor's life. So we began reading.

IN OUR MINISTRY—
WHAT ARE WE OCCUPIED WITH?

"LET US NOTE AT THE OUTSET that
there is little apparent difference between
ministry to the house and ministry to the Lord. Many of you are doing
your utmost to help your brethren, and you are laboring to save sinners
and administer the affairs of the church. But let me ask you: Have you
been seeking to meet the need around you, or have you been seeking to
serve the Lord? Is it your fellowmen you have in view, or is it HIM?

Let us be quite frank. Work for the Lord undoubtedly has its attract-
tions for the flesh. You may find it very interesting, and you may be
thrilled when crowds gather to hear you preach, and when numbers of
souls are saved. If you have to stay at home, occupied from morning to
night with mundane matters, then you think: How meaningless life is!
How grand it would be if I could go out and serve the Lord! If only I
were free to go around preaching, or even to talk to people about Him!

But that is not spirituality. That is merely a matter of natural prefer-
ence. Oh, if only we could see that very much work for God is not really

ministry to Him! He Himself has told us that there was a class of Levites who busily served in the Temple, and yet they were not (really) serving Him; they were merely serving the House. Service to the Lord and service to the House appear so much alike that it is often difficult to differentiate between the two.

If an Israelite came along to the Temple and wanted to worship God, those Levites would come to his aid and help him to offer his peace offering and his burnt offering. They would help him drag the sacrifice to the altar, and they would slay it. Surely that was a grand work to be engaged in, reclaiming sinners and leading believers closer to the Lord! And God took account of the service of those Levites who helped men bring their peace offerings and their burnt offerings to the altar. Yet He said it was not ministry unto HIMSELF.

Brothers and sisters, there is a heavy burden on my heart that you might realize what God is after. He wants ministers who will minister to Him. "They shall come near to ME to minister unto ME; and they shall stand before ME to offer unto ME the fat and the blood.. They shall minister unto ME" (Ezk. 44:16).

The thing I fear most is that many of you will go out and win sinners to the Lord and build up believers, without ministering to the Lord Himself. Much so called service for Him is simply following our own natural inclinations. We have such active dispositions that we cannot bear to stay at home, so we run around for our own relief. We may be serving sinners, and we may be serving believers, but we are all the time serv-our own flesh.

But what do we really mean when we talk of serving God or serving the Temple. Here is what the Word says:—"But the priests, the Levites, the sons of Zadok, that kept the charge of My sanctuary when the children of Israel went astray from Me, they shall come near to Me to minister unto Me; and they shall stand before Me to offer unto Me the fat and the blood, saith the Lord God" (vs 15).

In the sanctuary:
    Ministering unto the Lord.

In the outer court:
    Ministering unto the people

THE TWO CONDITIONS

The conditions basic to all ministry that can truly be called ministry to the Lord are —(1) drawing near to Him and (2) standing before Him. How hard we often find it to drag ourselves into His presence! We shrink from the solitude, and even when we do detach ourselves physically, our thoughts still keep wandering outside. Many of us can enjoy working among people, but how many of us can draw near to God in the Holy of Holies? Yet it is only as we draw near to Him that we can minister to Him. To come into the presence of God and kneel before Him for an hour demands all the strength we possess. We have to be violent to hold that ground. But every one who serves the Lord knows the preciousness of such times, the sweetness of waking at midnight and spending an hour in prayer, or waking very early in the morning and getting up for an hour of prayer.

Let me be very frank with you. Unless we really know what it is to draw near to God, we cannot know what it is to serve HIM. It is impossible to stand afar off and still minister to HIM. We cannot serve HIM from a distance. There is only one place where ministry to Him is possible and that is the Holy Place. In the outer court you approach the people; in the most Holy Place you approach the Lord.

IN APPROACHING THE LORD:

We learn how to stand before HIM;
We learn how to stand still;
We stand before HIM to await His will;
When we have learned to stand—we can MINISTER.

The passage we have quoted emphasizes the need of drawing near to God if we are to minister to HIM. It speaks also of standing before HIM to minister. It seems to me that today we always want to be moving on; we cannot stand still. There are so many things claiming our attention that we are perpetually on the go. We cannot stop for a moment. But a spiritual person knows how to stand still. He can stand before God till God makes His will known. He can stand and await orders.

Here I wish to address myself specifically to my fellow-workers. May I ask you: Is not all your work definitely organized and carried out to schedule? And has it not got to be done in great haste? Can you be persuaded to call a halt and not move for a little while? That is what is referred to here—"stand and minister to me."

None can truly minister to the Lord who do not know the meaning of this word: "They shall DRAW NIGH UNTO ME and minister unto Me." Nor can any minister to Him who do not understand this further word:

"They shall STAND BEFORE ME to minister unto ME." Brethren, do you not think any servant should await his master's orders before seeking to serve Him?

TWO TYPES OF SIN

There are two types of sin before God. One is the sin of rebelling against His commands, i.e. refusing to obey when He issues orders. The other is the sin of going ahead when the Lord has not issued orders. The one is rebellion; the other is presumption. The one is not doing what the Lord has required; the other is doing what the Lord has not required. Standing before the Lord deals with the sin of doing what the Lord has not commanded.

Brothers and sisters, how much of the work you have done has been based on the clear command of the Lord? How much have you done because of His direct instructions? And how much have you done simply on the ground that the thing you did was a good thing to do? Let me tell you that nothing so damages the Lord's interests as a "good thing." "Good things" are the greatest hindrance to the accomplishment of His Will. The moment we are faced with anything wicked or unclean, we immediately recognize it as a thing the Christian ought to avoid, and for that reason things which are positively evil are not such a menace to the Lord's purpose as "good things." You think: This thing would not be wrong, or, that thing is the very best that could be done; so you go ahead and do it without stopping to inquire if it is the Will of God. Oh, we who are His children all know that we ought not to do anything evil, but we think that if only our conscience does not forbid a thing, or if a thing commends itself to us as positively good, that is reason enough to go ahead and do it.

That thing you contemplate doing may be very good, but are you standing before the Lord, awaiting His command regarding it? "They shall stand before Me" involves halting in His presence and refusing to move till He issues His orders. Ministry to the Lord means that. In the outer court it is human need that governs. Just let someone come along to sacrifice an ox or a sheep, and there is work for you to do. But in the Holiest Place there is utter solitude. Not a soul comes in. No brother or sister governs us here, nor does any committee determine our affairs. In the Holiest Place there is one authority only, the authority of the Lord. If He appoints me a task I do it; if He appoints me no task I do none.

But something is required of us as we stand before the Lord and minister to HIM. We are required to offer Him "the fat and the blood." The blood answers the demands of His holiness and righteousness; the fat meets the requirements of His glory. The blood deals with the question of our sin; the fat deals with the question of HIS SATISFACTION. The blood removes all that belongs to the old creation; the fat brings in the new. And this is something more than spiritual doctrine. Our soul-life was involved in the pouring out of HIS soul unto death. When He shed His eternally incorruptible blood, He was not only pouring out His own life, He was pouring out the whole of the life man had by natural birth. And He not only died: He arose from the dead, and "the life that He lives unto God," He lives for God's satisfaction. He offers "the fat and the blood." We too, who would minister to the Lord, must offer the fat and the blood. And that impossible thing is possible on the basis of what He has done.

But such ministry is confined to a certain place, "They shall enter into My sanctuary, and they shall come near to My table to minister unto Me, and they shall keep My charge" (vs 16). Ministry that is "unto Me" is in the inner sanctuary, in the hidden place, not in the outer court exposed to public view. People may think we are doing nothing, but service to God within the Holy Place far transcends service to the people in the outer court. (God's yardstick for evaluating is so different from ours.) Brothers and Sisters, let us learn what it means to stand before the Lord awaiting His orders, serving at His command only, and governed by no consideration but the consideration of His Will.

The same passage tells us how they must be clothed who would minister to the Lord. "They shall be clothed with linen garments; and no wool shall come upon them, whiles they minister in the gates of the inner court, and within. They shall have linen bonnets upon their heads, and shall have linen breeches upon their loins." Those who minister to the Lord may not wear wool, Why not? The reason is given below: "They shall not gird themselves with anything that causeth sweat." No work that produces sweat is acceptable to the Lord. But what does "sweat" signify? We all know that the first occasion when sweat is mentioned was when Adam was driven from the Garden of Eden. After Adam had sinned, God pronounced this sentence upon him: "Cursed is the ground for thy sake; in toil shalt thou eat of it all the days of thy life... in the sweat of thy face shalt thou eat bread" (Gen. 3:17-19).

It is clear that sweat is a condition of the curse. Because the curse rested on the ground it ceased to yield its fruit without man's effort, and such effort produced sweat. When the blessing of God is withheld, fleshly effort becomes necessary, and that causes sweat. All work that produces sweat is positively prohibited to those who minister to the Lord. Yet today what an expenditure of energy there is in any work for Him! Alas! few Christians can do any work today without sweating over it. Their work involves planning and scheming, exhorting and urging, and very much running around. It cannot be done without a great deal of fleshly zeal. Nowadays if there is no sweat, there is no work. Before work for God can be undertaken there is a great deal of rushing to and fro making numerous contacts, having consultations and discussions, and finally getting the approval of various people before going ahead.

69

As for waiting quietly in the presence of God and seeking His instructions, that is out of the question. Yet in spiritual work the one factor to be taken into account is God. The one Person to make contact with is God. Oh! that is the preciousness of spiritual work—it is related to God. And in relation to Him there is work to do, but it is work that produces no sweat (carnal energy). If we have to advertize the work and use great effort to promote it, then it is obvious that it does not spring from prayer in the presence of God. Please bear with me when I say that all work which is truly spiritual is done in the presence of God. If you really work in God's presence, when you come into the presence of men they will respond. You will not have to use endless means in order to help them. Spiritual work is God's work, and when God works man does not need to expend so much effort that he 'sweats over it'.''

I love to read in Acts 13 about the prophets and teachers in the church at Antioch, that "as they ministered to the Lord and fasted, the Holy Ghost said: Separate Me Barnabas and Saul for the work whereunto I have called them.'' We see there the one principle that governs work for God in the New Testament dispensation. The Holy Spirit only commissions men to the work as they are ministering to the Lord. Unless ministry to the Lord is the thing that governs us, the work will be confusing. In the beginning of the church's history in Antioch, the Holy Spirit said: "Separate Me Barnabas and Saul for the work whereunto I have called them.'' God does not want volunteers for His work; He wants conscripts. He will not have you preaching the Gospel just because you want to. The work of the Lord is suffering serious damage today at the hand of volunteers; it lacks those who can say as He did: "He that sent me . . .'' Brothers and Sisters, the work of God is God's own work, and not work that you can take up at your pleasure. Neither churches, nor missionary societies, nor evangelistic bands can send men to work for God. The authority to commission men is not in the hands of men, but solely in the hands of the Spirit of God.

When God could find no way to bring all the Levites to the place of ministry to Himself, He chose the sons of Zadok from among them for this special service. Why did He select the sons of Zadok? Because, when the Children of Israel went astray, they recognized that the outer court had been irreparably corrupted, so they did not seek to preserve it; but they made it their business to preserve the sanctity of the Holy Place.

Brothers and sisters, can you bear to let the external structure go, or must you persist in putting up a scaffolding to preserve it? It is the Holy Place God is out to preserve — a place utterly set apart for Him, a place where the standard is absolute. Oh! I beseech you before God to hear His call to forsake the outer court and devote yourself to His service in the holy place.'' (From *Ministry to the House or to the Lord*).

THIS MOTHER DISCOVERED THE DIFFERENCE!

For several years I was perplexed! I stood with my teen age son continually beseeching God to help him, yet in spite of all my counsel and praying, he seemed to increase his rebellion and reckless escapades.

Then a change came! One night God revealed what it would mean for me to be identified with Him in a new position. Suddenly I realized how fleshly mother-ties had colored all my praying; therefore I was not so much concerned for God as for my son and how his behavior affected me. I saw how, as a typical mother with her outspread protective wings, I was seeking to shield my son from harm or danger, even to shield him from anything God might need to allow to awaken Him. I had always been identified (standing with) my son instead of God.

Then God used the Cross as a great scissor and asked for permission to cut these fleshly ties that I might be released from standing with my son. It was like taking a big move—away from him over into the heart of God. I saw how this new identification might involve great cost to me. If I began praying from this new position, I should be willing for any course necessary to bring my boy to God. I sensed my relation with him seemed different.

The next night when he was leaving to go out for a thrilling time with his friends, I called him aside: "Son, I have something important to tell you. I want you to know that mother loves you, even more than I have been able to show. But I am no longer praying that God will spare you from harm when you race with the boys. I am no longer standing with you—beseeching God in your behalf! From now on I am standing with God for His purpose and plan in your life. In His stead I beseech you to turn from your wild ways and yield to God."

The boy pretended he was unconcerned and left the house with that typical teen age attitude: "So what—who cares." But he could not get away from mother's haunting words. How they penetrated as words had never cut before. Mother spoke with a new authority! There was something different in her eye. Did she really love God more than him? The young son tried to enjoy his reckless times with the gang, but mother's words and look kept haunting him.

One whole month passed. Mother was different! She didn't nag, didn't scold, she simply walked with a new confidence as though God was working. And He was.

We must omit many details, but it was only a short time before a crisis brought that boy to know God for Himself, not merely for himself. Today he is a veteran soldier of the Cross on the mission field. It all happened because mother had learned the secret of...

MINISTERING FROM A
NEW POSITION

THERE IS A DIFFERENCE! Either we are *standing with man beseeching God* to act in his behalf, or we are *standing with God beseeching man* to respond to God's offer of grace. As we have pictured (in the diagram) it is a matter of position and approach. As long as we are yet man-centered in position we are ministering with ourselves identified with man. But when we are truly God-centered we are ministering identified with God. In the first we are *moving unto the Lord;* while, in the latter we are *moving out from the Lord* to the people.

All that is really involved in this glorious distinction will not be understood unless we grasp what Paul is saying in 2 Cor. 3, 4 and 5. The mother, whose testimony we have shared at the beginning, had found the difference between being identified with her son and being identified with God. With Paul she could now announce: "Seeing we have THIS MINISTRY ... we faint not" (2 Cor. 4:1). In these three chapters, Paul is picturing a spiritual identification with the Lord in oneness of mind, purpose, vision and authority. Those who have passed through union in death and resurrection are no longer "living unto themselves but unto Him." They know what it is to abide with Him in the most holy place. Now as they move forth, they understand the "word of reconciliation" which has been committed to them. As ambassadors they move out from His presence to stand in His stead boldly beseeching men to be reconciled (2 Cor. 5:19-20).

Oh, I hope you catch this difference in ministry. Who are you beseeching? Where do you stand? If you are still concerned merely for man and his welfare, you will be pleading to God for help. But once you have embraced the heart and vision of God, you will be pleading with man that God might realize His full purpose.

We remember Moses (Exod. 32) was in the presence of the Lord when the people made the golden calf. As God communicated to him all that was taking place down at the foot of the mountain, Moses immediately began beseeching God on behalf of the people. But it was not for long,

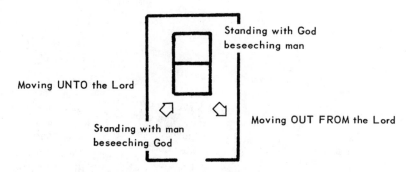

Standing with God
beseeching man

Moving UNTO the Lord

Standing with man
beseeching God

Moving OUT FROM the Lord

because His identification with the Lord in His purpose and plan allowed him to move forth unto the people to beseech them to turn from their rebellion.

As we have seen in Moses and the mother, we shall also see that in the sons of Zadok there are three things which are by-products in every life which ministers unto the Lord: discernment, authority and contentment.

Turn to Ezekiel 44 and we will see this in the ministry of the sons of Zadok. First, as they came forth from the holy place, they had the ability to teach the people the difference between the holy and the profane (vs 23). Everyone who has remained in His presence has a peculiar spiritual discernment operating. They have an inner ear for knowing whether music is simply soulish, entertaining or truly God honoring in a service. In the ministry of the Word they sense the difference between mere second-hand knowledge and personal revelation.

Second, as the sons of Zadok moved out from God's presence they were endowed with authority to stand in judgment when controversy arose (vs 24). There is something unique about that authority which is God-imparted, not delegated by man. How often in a time of crisis we have seen folk turn for counsel, not to the elected elders, but to one who has been hidden away with the Lord—one who has spiritual authority instead of official authority.

Third, the sons of Zadok were to have no (material) possession in Israel. God says of them, "I am their inheritance; I am their possession" (vs 28). Here we discover the amazing contentment which accompanies this ministry. It is wholly unnecessary for God to reward these dedicated ministers with "things." One who has chosen to bring satisfaction to God (in the fat) has already become wholly satisfied with just HIM—and has already found his inheritance. He needs no worldly estate. Rather he accepts with thanksgiving the blessings which come to him as by-products of a ministry unto the Lord.

What is more needful today than this effective ministry—to be moving out from the Lord with His discernment, His authority and His contentment?

THIS PASTOR EXPLAINS;

I have found a new ministry! Since I have learned to minister unto HIM in the Holy Place there has come a oneness of vision and purpose. Now I can move out to the people with a new authority, yet with a greater compassion for them. And what is more wonderful—when I know I am standing identified with Him—what confidence there is in speaking as His ambassador with portfolio. For the first time I am beginning to appreciate the unique prayers and ministry of the apostle Paul. It seems so many ministries have hardly reached the Old Testament level—but now to enjoy this New Testament privilege of living in the viewpoint of God is to move in tune with His throbbing heart. Indeed Paul's was an ultimate ministry, and I am also longing . . . . . .

TO PARTICIPATE IN

THIS ULTIMATE MINISTRY

ON A FEW OCCASIONS you have met some servant of God who was utterly different. What made him so? You sensed a real pull in your spirit to also live dangerously and courageously, but you could not. You were even troubled because he seemed so much more concerned for God's interests than for your blessing! Let us see if we can understand what makes him different.

We have previously considered those sons of Zadok who were privileged to move into the first room of the sanctuary to minister unto the the Lord. There were also those other priests whose conduct only permitted them to minister in the outer court. All were priests after the order of Levi who enjoyed a divine service as they ministered in the earthly sanctuary. However wonderful and glorious that ministry was, it had certain limitations. Because the blood of bulls and goats could only cover, not cleanse away sin, no priest (even the sons of Zadok) could enter into the most holy place. (There was one exception—once a year the high priest went into the most holy place). Now since Calvary we can enjoy something much better. God's perfect Lamb has shed perfect blood and the way into the most holy place has been opened. Once a purged conscience was not possible, but now through perfect blood, through the new and living way, we are invited to enter into the most holy place to function in a ministry after the order of Melchisedec. Instead of mere divine service (Heb. 9:1) which was in the earthly sanctuary, we are to function in a spiritual service pertaining to the heavenly sanctuary. In this new ministry, instead of functioning with mere earthly shadows and symbols, we enjoy a heavenly reality.

EARTHLY PRIESTHOOD	ROYAL PRIESTHOOD
Levitical ministry	Melchisedec ministry
Heb. 9:1	1 Pet. 2:5

"divine service". . . . . "spiritual service"
"wordly sanctuary" . . . . "spiritual house"

In this former ministry there was a functioning with mere earthly shadows and symbols, but now.	In this new ministry we enjoy the heavenly reality—the fulfillment in Christ, Himself.
The Spirit was with them to enable divine service, but there was no indwelling union.	Now the Holy Spirit dwells within; therefore we are "joined in one spirit" and can enjoy a spiritual service.

As we have pictured (in the diagram) there is a very real difference between the Levitical and the Melchisedec ministry. Previously the Holy Spirit had been with the Old Testament saints to guide, to direct and to equip them. He had come upon them in power and authority for service. Now, since the Holy place is opened , and man is allowed to enter in, we can enjoy a vital union with the Lord. God says we are "joined in one spirit" which means a complete spiritual union or identification with the Lord. Now the Holy Spirit has come to dwell in the human spirit (our most holy place). For this reason our ministry is not merely an earthly ministry of divine service, but ours has become a royal ministry of spiritual service. Peter writes that as a holy priesthood we are to "offer up spiritual sacrifices acceptable to God . . . " (1 Peter 2:5).

It would seem perhaps the great majority of servants today have not even reached that level of ministry which the sons of Zadok enjoyed—a ministry in the first room which is wholly unto the Lord. But Paul would let no one remain there, however glorious. There is a better ministry. Instead of merely *moving unto the Lord*, we can now enter into a vital union with Him and He will thrust us forth to represent Him. Thus when we move out from the Lord, it is with a peculiar discernment, a unique authority and an amazing contentment. Like Moses—whose ministry typified the Melchisedec—we shall bear upon our faces the glory of the ONE we minister to others. Such a ministry is more than instrumental *for God*, it is EXPRESSIVE OF GOD.

An Indian legend tells of a tribe which lived in a great forest at the foot of a lofty mountain peak. One day the old chief summoned the lads of the tribe to his side and called upon them to clamber to the top of the lofty summit and win the renown of its conquest. This would test their mettle and prove their worth to the tribe, for it had been many a moon since a young brave had mastered the sky-piercing pinnacle. The braves obeyed. Hours went by and they began to return. One brought a tuft of moss torn from the mountain side, a token only accessible from a lofty height. Presently another came with the broken twig of a tree which stood still higher up the mountain, but yet not upon its summit. By and by came another grasping a beautiful flower which grew well up toward the top of the peak, but still not upon its top. All the lads were back save one. For hours he delayed. But as the gloom of the night begun to fall, they heard his voice calling in the distant forest. Nearer and nearer he came until he stepped into the fire-lit circle of the waiting camp. He had no token in his hand but when they saw his face they did not need to ask him if he had conquered the towering peak. For there was a certain light in his face and his eyes shone gloriously as he cried aloud, "I have seen the crystal sea!"

So it will be with all who participate in this ultimate ministry. The emphasis is not on WHAT THEY DO but on WHAT THEY ARE. People always recognize one who has lived in His presence, one who has glimpsed the crystal sea of Eternal Truth: God HIMSELF. When such a one moves out to minister, his authority is not legal but spiritual, his sacrifices are not symbols but reality, he shares more than knowledge— he shares CHRIST.

> While I am still man-centered
> I am merely ministering for God.
> But as I become truly God-centered
> He is through me ministering to man.

THE

ULTIMATE

PROMOTION

WILLING TO HONESTLY RECOGNIZE
THE LUST OF POSITION-SEEKING

WHAT GOVERNS REJECTION OR
PROMOTION BY THE LORD?

WHAT IS THE SOURCE
OF TRUE HONOR?

We Must Also Learn

Of course it all appeared as a "divine coincidence" to Jonah that a Tarshishian ship should be waiting in the harbor, that he should have the exact fare in his pocket, and that he was already packed and there on that very day it was leaving. Coincidence? Surely! "All things work together"—he must have smiled.

Yet inwardly his heart kept taunting him. How could God expect him to move down to Ninevah —he, a Jew, moving in among those awful Gentiles. Is it not right that every move by a pastor should be to a "larger work" — that each move should be a "promotion." Ninevah seemed to be just the opposite. Would God really ask such?

Now our ancient Jonah has many a modern counterpart. Like that prophet of old, *modern Jonah* has often warned that there is "that which is highly esteemed among men" and yet "is abomination in the sight of God." He has often said "a servant of God, following his own desire and counsel, may move into a 'larger work,' but actually be taking a smaller place in the plan of God." Further, he has always insisted that "true promotion" is of God and sometimes may take on the appearance of that which is quite contrary to man's estimate. But when the hour of personal testing comes, what will he do? Follow Jonah or take Philip as his example.

You recall how Philip was taken from a large and successful ministry at Samaria to minister to one man in the desert! If Philip had any notions about the advisability of such a shift of location they are not recorded, and they certainly were subjected to the will of God, for "he rose and went." GOD SAID, "Move." That, and that alone, is sufficient reason for the servant of God to move on to a new field.

Now Jonah was already having heart trouble, but the boat was much too far out for Jonah to swim back. The first lesson from Jonah we must not miss is this: There are some prisons which are not visible to the naked eye. The boat may have seemed like a prison, and the accommodations he would soon have in a submarine hotel for a season may have been as a dark jail — but actually Jonah was already in the first and most terrible prison: LOCKED UP IN THE CELL OF A WICKED HEART THAT IS SELFISHLY BENT ON MANEUVERING ITS PROMOTION.

**

A PASTOR ASKS:

There are those times when I question whether my attitude and conception are right. In recent years I have experienced the deep working of the Cross in a very radical adjustment in my life and ministry. It has (I believe) turned me from the selfish seeking of position and honor. I think I have become content in allowing God to work through me instead of ambitiously promoting my own little kingdom.

Then when I look around at my fellow-laborers in the ministry who seem to be a success, I begin to wonder. I see so many who are producing some private exhibition of their labors, or carving out some little kingdom which will grant them a position and honor. Others are grasping for some new experience or teaching, some new method or technique for enhancing their ministry. To me, this savors of the "inordinate" or of mere "opportunism."

Now this is my concern. How can I keep from my proneness to a critical spirit when I discern selfish promotion and selfish methods? Perhaps what I have experienced of the Cross working in me is just enough to make me miserable, but not triumphant in the "ways of the Lord." I seek to honestly recognize whether I might be jealous of another's apparent success because I have seemingly little visible fruit. Perhaps my real trouble is that I am not wholly free from the lust of position-seeking.

WILLING TO HONESTLY RECOGNIZE THE LUST OF POSITION-SEEKING

THERE IS AN INNER REST! There comes an inner confidence once we learn that no man need advance himself or promote his own cause. God will advance and promote in His own time and His own way. The prophet Samuel well understood this and rehearsed it before Israel one day: "...It is the Lord that advanced Moses and Aaron..." (1 Sam. 12:6). Again the Psalmist (75:7) gives similar exhortation: "But God...

putteth down one and setteth up another."

We do well to recognize that a very real conflict is raging in almost every breast until God gives light and adjustment at the Cross. We must first understand that in the beginning (at man's creation) God wove into man's very being a legitimate desire. God has designed every man so as to give him a built-in desire to fulfill destiny and purpose, and to thereby find meaning to life. It was imperative to man's very personality that he should sense worth, value and importance of life in fulfilling his calling and in achieving worthwhile goals and endeavors. Therefore this longing and insatiable urge to find position and to receive honor from achievement is innate in every man. Let no one foolishly imagine that he can ignore this divine imprint within every personality. It is a built-in desire intended by God. Man must become important to God so as to fulfill this sense of worth and value in life.

But here is man's difficulty, so often overlooked. When the first man, Adam, chose an independent course, it was to fulfill his own desire and purpose all apart from God and upon a line wholly contrary to God's way of working. This original built-in desire which was proper has now, through the Fall, developed into a perverted desire. Every man "in Adam" has followed the same perversion: the lust of position-seeking and the grasping for greatness and importance for himself — all apart from God and His eternal purpose. Now one might expect to find this inordinate lust and perverted desire compelling *men of the world* to grasp for honor, fame, popularity and position, but when this effort at self-promotion hides itself in *religious garb and spiritual zeal*, it seems almost unthinkable.

We must learn two things: (1) to recognize the need of every personality to fulfill his worth and value, and (2) to recognize God's way of promoting and honoring man. But we must also understand how God, by the Cross, has dealt a death-blow to this perverted lust of position-seeking. Henceforth man can be set free to fulfill *in God's way*, the original intention for his life.

All Scripture seems to teach this simple truth: God purposes to *prepare man before* He gives him position. Man always seeks position first without experiencing the divine preparation necessary for that position. Let us consider first man's way and then God's way. Was not this perverted method evident in James and John when they sought the right and left hand position in the Kingdom? Their attitude reflects the typical way of man's position-seeking. It was the lust to *become* something great *before they became* something in their inner being. Jesus quickly reminded them that there was a twofold preparation (a union in His death and a sharing in His cup) before they could expect to sit in this favored position at His right or left hand. But they hardly understood that *first they must be prepared vessels before they could enjoy this prepared position.* First they must know the preparation of the Cross and then suffering.

Here then is God's way of promotion. In Joseph we see how God used the long years of imprisonment, suffering and testing to inwardly prepare him for the throne and the honor in Egypt. How different is God's way of giving position *in due time* as compared with man's way of grasping position before the time.

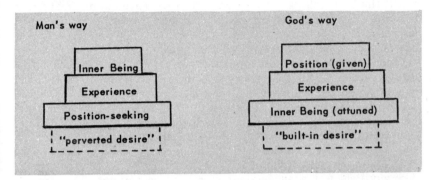

Man's way

Inner Being

Experience

Position-seeking

"perverted desire"

God's way

Position (given)

Experience

Inner Being (attuned)

"built-in desire"

Thus we have pictured (in the diagram) two ways of building our life-work. When man builds (without first the work and preparation of the Cross in him) he seeks position first and then hopes through experience to finally come to a development of character in his inner being. But this is backward and folly. God seeks first a vital union with man's inner being. Then He enrolls him in His schoolroom of experience. Through sharing His wisdom and knowledge, man is finally prepared for and receives the position God intends for his life. Of course God increases the position as man's experience and preparation increases.

We look at another life who knew this and he said: "Through wisdom is an house builded; and by understanding it is established" (Prov. 24:3). How well Solomon knew that God must prepare the heart and bring the inner being into harmony with Himself. In 1 Kings 3:1-13 we read how he considered himself as a mere child who needed so much to depend wholly upon God for wisdom and understanding to reign over Israel—"so great a people."

While we read about it, we must be sure we have fully learned this important lesson: All true promotion *comes from God,* not from man. The Psalmist said: "For promotion cometh neither from the east, nor from the west, nor from the south" (Psalm 75:6). Let us ask, why did he omit the north? Is it not because throughout Scripture God is pictured as inhabiting the north! Satan in his proud exclamation announced that he would ascend into heaven... exalt his throne above the stars of God... sit ALSO upon the mount of the congregation,"... IN THE SIDES OF THE NORTH" (Isa. 14:13). It is no secret, for most students of the Word agree that God is pictured as inhabiting the north. So we can be assured then – that promotion will come from the north. The Psalmist continues in the next verse: "But God is the judge: He putteth down one and setteth up another."

In answering what the pastor mentioned at the beginning, we might say this: There is an inner contentment which comes from God when we know our motive is single—one of pleasing Him and living only to fulfill His high calling for our lives. When we move out of "rest" it is because we begin to accept man's pregmatic yardstick for measuring success. The moment we seek to compare or evaluate our ministry with others and in the light of our own understanding we are wrong.

Paul reminds us we are called to be *faithful,* not successful by men's yardstick. He continues: "...it is a very small thing that I should be judged (or evaluated) of you, or of man's judgment: yea, I judge not mine own self" (1 Cor. 4:3). That is, Paul is insisting that he cannot properly evaluate his own ministry right now in the light of eternity. "Therefore judge (evaluate) nothing before the time..." (vs. 5), that is, before God puts the proper light and perspective upon the work in the light of eternity.

Surely Paul was misunderstood by his contemporaries. They thought he was biggoted and unreasonable in wanting to appeal his case to Caesar and to become a prisoner when he might be free for his greatest ministry. There he was, considering himself a prisoner of Jesus Christ (not of Rome) rotting away in a prison when he could, they imagined, be at the height of his ministry, planting new churches and further establishing those already founded. Yes, how narrow is man's perspective *in time.* Who could have looked down the centuries to our present hour to realize how the letters Paul wrote while in prison would become of far greater spiritual importance than perhaps a thousand churches he might have founded? Who, but God, could see this greater ministry and thus give to Paul that inner sense of fulfillment and confidence that he was truly living in the full measure of eternal value and worth?

Seek not for promotion now – nor attempt to judge spiritual things now. God's promise is "then shall every man have praise of God...."

WE LITTLE KNOW HOW GOOD AND NECESSARY IT IS FOR US TO HAVE ADVERSARIES, AND FOR HERETICS TO HOLD UP THEIR HEADS AGAINST US.
MARTIN LUTHER.

SOMEONE HAS MADE the complaint: "There are times
when it seems that some men get all the breaks, while others
get only knocks." Is this really true? Surely we can recognize that this is a natural man's observation which stems
from an inner spirit of antagonism toward God. It is like
saying that God *is* a respecter of persons and shows par-
tiality and favoritism in His rejecting of one and promoting
another at will. How shall we answer such charges? There is
one thing we must understand if we would know . . .

WHAT GOVERNS REJECTION OR
PROMOTION BY THE LORD.

IN SAUL AND DAVID we have two men
in contrast. One goes down in rejection
while the other is selected for promotion. What really made the difference in Saul and David? We shall not answer this until the end, but
let us simply say at this point that we must recognize and distinguish
between God's moral and sovereign action.

In King Saul we have the graphic portrayal of what happens when
men assume position on their own, apart from God's choosing and
preparation. In David we see God's way of preparation *first* and *then*
the giving of position.

You will recall that for years Israel had enjoyed God's rule over them through the voice of the prophet Samuel. Why then did they cry out for a change? In wanting to be like the nations around them, they began begging God for a king who would rule over them and lead them into battle. It is true that in due time God would have given them the king *He was preparing* for the kingdom. Now in their rebellion they are actually rejecting God's reign over them, and instead setting up Saul to reign. Notice how clearly Samuel warns them:

> "And Samuel said unto all Israel. Behold, I have harkened *unto your voice* in all that ye said unto me, and have made a king over you. And when *ye saw* that Nahas the king of the children of Ammon came against you, ye said unto me, Nay; but a king shall reign over us: when the Lord your God was your king. Now therefore behold the king *whom ye have desired!...*" (1 Sam. 12:1, 12, 13).

Note carefully the phrases: "whom ye have chosen" and "whom ye have desired." It was not God's first will or first best, yet in their continued begging, He grants them their request. What a lesson this should teach us! Because God may grant a request does not imply that it is His highest. When they lusted for meat in the wilderness we read that, "...He granted their request...but sent leanness...." So God grants Israel's request, but Samuel reminds them, "...behold, the Lord hath set a king over you." But, as you have been warned, "He will take your sons...your vineyards...your sheep..." (1 Sam. 8:11-17).

Even though it was never His intention *to give Saul as king,* nor was it *His time* for the kingdom to be established, yet He allowed them — even stood with Saul — when they had chosen him as their king. This is because God honors the importance of government. He will recognize the position of a husband, a governor, a pastor or a king even though He knows they have not been duly prepared for the position.

Here is the important lesson: God does not reject a man whom the people may have given position until He has given that one every chance to prove himself and become established. Nor will He allow men to reject the one whom they have given position, even when the man through repeated failure demonstrates that he was not yet prepared for the position. How fickle are men; one day they will exalt and the next day they will crucify that same man. God, through Samuel reminds Israel:

> "If ye will fear the Lord, and serve Him, and obey His voice, and not rebel against the commandment of the Lord, then shall both ye and also the king that reigneth over you continue following the Lord your God" (vs. 14).

Thus Israel in the midst of warning, gets her way, and Saul is given a position. How quickly we shall see that there has never been any *inward preparation* of his heart to fear the Lord and lead His people. He has never been enrolled in God's special school room of heart preparation and experience. Saul discovers too late how precarious is his position. What a thing to be placed on the stage before the eyes of all the people—*there* to learn the lesson which should have been learned in secret *before* the position was given. Now Saul must learn experience through crisis and pressure in order to come to an inward heart preparation before God. God would have started with this heart-preparation if things had followed His own way.

God gave Saul every opportunity to prove himself and to be established before the people. A moral God who is no respecter of persons could not reject a man until he had proved himself utterly unworthy. God will give Saul—in fact every man—this same right. But we see what happens to an unprepared, undisciplined king under pressure. In the very first crisis when Saul is leading the army against the Philistines, we read: "... and all the people followed him (Saul) trembling..." (Ch. 13:7). What a picture! A man in position but without experience or inner preparation! When people follow any leader in whom there is no established confidence, what else can be expected but fear and trembling? It is, however, a predicament of their own making. Without foundation work in Saul's inner being, without development or experience, it is little wonder that we read in vs. 8, "... and the people were scattered from him."

They had chosen their own king, and now they were fearful of following him. They sensed Saul's inner tremble—and they trembled and scattered. When Samuel did not come with divine help, what else could a weakling do? Saul testified: "I forced myself, and offered a burnt offering" (vs. 12).

What had been God's purpose in this crisis? Samuel tells Saul: "... Thou hast done foolishly: thou hast not kept the commandment of the Lord... for now would the Lord have established thy kingdom upon Israel forever" (vs. 13). Thus we see the way the Lord would have established Saul in his position as king. Now in this failure Samuel reminds Saul, "... the Lord hath sought Him a man after His own heart..." Let us remember these are the words of the Lord *to Saul;* as yet the people do not know, nor are they free to reject Saul from his position.

Next we see in chapter 14 further failure and lack. Saul, as a typical undisciplined and unprepared leader makes a brash statement which he cannot fulfill. Once again he is put to open shame when the people side with Jonathan and refuse to allow the king to fulfill his word. Finally in chapter 15 we see Saul's failure in full obedience as he spares King Agag of the Amalekites, and of course allows the people to spare the best of the sheep and oxen for sacrifice.

What a lesson we see in all of this. A king who continually spares himself, can do no other than allow his people to spare themselves. Is it not true that our outward softness toward circumstances is but the reflection of our inner softness toward self? God says, "it is enough"; and we hear these final words to Saul:

> "For rebellion is as the sin of witchcraft... Because thou hast rejected the word of the Lord, He hath also REJECTED THEE FROM BEING KING" (1 Sam. 15:23).

What finality! Henceforth God will regard Saul's position as king no longer and David will be anointed king.

Now before closing, we must answer our first question. What really governed the rejection of Saul? Even though he was the people's choice God does not reject Saul until he has proven himself to be wholly unworthy and incapable. A moral God could do no less: He could not reject merely out of His own arbitrary whims. Of course, from the beginning God knew the end of Saul. With God there is a fore-knowledge which precedes His sovereign will. Whomever He uses in dishonor and whomever He hardeneth—He has beforehand known what course they would choose. Thus every man who stands before a righteous and sovereign God can only exclaim: "God you have done what was right—I have no basis for excusing myself." Nor can King Saul.

When one man "seems" to get only breaks and another only knocks, we must be careful lest we be guilty of interpreting according to our narrow sliver of light and judging Him who lives in the broad-daylight where He sees and knows all. How often we have been shut up to that verse in 2 Chronicles 16:9:

> "The eyes of the Lord run to and fro throughout the whole earth, to shew Himself strong in the behalf of them whose heart is perfect toward Him...."

Is this perhaps the one basic difference which God saw between Saul and David? God saw in David an opportunity to "shew Himself strong." Thus we can understand God's sovereign selection of David. Of course we are not told, yet there is this evidence in God's working, that surely it is His foreknowledge more than any arbitrary whim, which causes Him to show mercy on whom He will show mercy and to show compassion on whom He will show compassion. I know what the extremists will say, but I can only concur with Paul's words: "Is God unrighteous? God forbid!" (Rom. 1:14).

Of course we are careful to make this distinction: There are some things which God does simply because it is morally right. That is, His working in moral correctness. Yet there are other times we see Him as a Father who chooses one child above another simply out of the good pleasure of His will. It is not necessarily that He loves one above another or even that He does it for any particular reason. Even an earthly father will simply make a sovereign selection of a son to help him realize some purpose.

So it was with David. He was chosen from among many brothers simply by God's sovereign selection. We have no reason given for this selection. We only know that God could look down the corridor of time— long before David was born—and choose to set him apart from his mother's womb unto that glorious position as the unifier and great King of Israel. Thus we understand this inward preparation in David from the very beginning. God had very early enrolled him in His own special school room that He might work first in his inner being a preparation of heart, then bring him through those experiences which would qualify him for the position of king. Thus it was that God had been doing an inner establishing long before David was to be *in due time* established outwardly as King. We have seen *man's way* in Saul: working from the outer—hoping to establish the inner—and the top falls to the bottom. But then we have seen *God's way:* working from the inner to the outer —from the bottom to the top.

"LOOK ON THINE OWN NOTHINGNESS AND BE HUMBLE, BUT LOOK AT JESUS, THY GREAT REPRE- SENTATIVE, AND BE GLAD. IT WILL SAVE THEE MANY PANGS IF THOU WILT LEARN TO THINK OF THYSELF AS BEING *IN HIM*."

C. H. SPURGEON.

THE SOURCE OF
TRUE HONOR!

T HERE ARE THOSE who might counsel this pastor to "get out of a church system" which produces such a squeeze. But where would he escape and not face a situation which is much the same in principle? What we are here concerned with is a problem much deeper than the church-system in which one is involved. It is first of all a question of allowing God to *take us through* to His end — allowing God to *make the outward position* we hold to be evidence of an *inward position.* Let us see what that means.

There are, perhaps, multitudes who have learned this lesson in one way or another. They are in the position which God has either allowed or placed them. Now they can do either of two things: run and seek an easier place (which really does not exist) or stand firm and allow God to do His own perfect work.

Mentioned above is an unusual pastor, in that he refuses to fall into the modern tradition of "running under pressure." But have we not all

88

seen this same problem in the home, in the school or in business? Even with those who have been given a position for which they are prepared and worthy, there will usually come a time of "civil war." Thus one's position will always be challenged, but as he learns to stand — God will both establish and bring forth true honor.

Let us once again observe this in the life of King David. Even after Saul's death and David's being received as king by Judah, there is a period of civil war. The eleven tribes of Israel had given their allegiance to Saul's son, Ishbosheth, while only the house of Judah followed David as their king.

In the bitter civil war which ensues we discover how God is not only working in David but is also purging the kingdom, until finally Israel also comes to anoint David as their king. "Thus David's power (and honor) kept increasing for the Lord of hosts was with him" (Berkeley — 1 Chron. 11:9).

Now let us observe something of the pattern we can expect: It is one thing for God to give one a position; it is still another thing for the people to accept and recognize that one as being in God's position. It is during this time of waiting for the people to recognize what God recognizes, that so many servants stumble and begin to wonder if God has forsaken them. It means learning to stand in the midst of conflict, in the midst of contrary winds unmoved, established and fixed on the foundation the Lord has given.

But once again we must make sure we are on that TRUE FOUNDATION. There is one sure mark we can always expect in those who are upon God's Foundation. It is humility. This is the first real virtue which will be developed in the inner being that is truly established on Christ as THE FOUNDATION. It would seem that this is *the cement* which welds our inner being to Him.

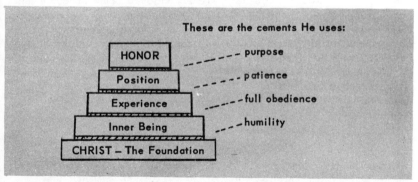

But we must see how there are other kinds of cement which are necessary in the building of the various levels: We have started with *humility* as the cement which binds our inner being to Christ: THE FOUNDATION. Consider how *full obedience* works as the cement to make experience valuable and meaningful. Because King Saul failed in full obedience, the experiences and crises were for naught. Yet they could have been the means by which God would have brought him to position. Then let us look at another cement with which God binds experience to position. We have seen when *patience* has had her perfect work that in due time God gives position.

Finally, we must ask what is the cement which will fasten our capstone (honor) to position. It is *our purpose.* Only when the position we have been given is wholly used for Him — when our single purpose is to realize God's intention — can we expect to share in His honor. Likewise if our purpose is to use position for our own end, true honor will vanish.

What an inner rest! What a complete assurance and confidence we have once we have learned to cooperate with the Master Architect. *Our one purpose is His honor.* To know that it is God who builds, God who advances and God who, in due time, allows us to share in His own honor — this is the vision and purpose we need.

OUR REAL PURPOSE IS REVEALING

When you have truly uncovered which foundation your life is built upon — self or Christ — you have a very real revelation of your purpose or controlling philosophy of life. There is such a difference! Either you are seeking *escape or fulfillment!* Lot's wife was interested only in escaping *from* Sodom for *her own sake,* while "just Lot" seemed pointed unto that fulfillment which God might yet realize through his life in spite of the many wasted, selfish years.

Are you plagued with trouble and pressure in the position God has given you? What are you really seeking? Is it *deliverance or development?* It would seem if you have already enjoyed some of God's inner preparation for that position, that you will surely *seek more development rather than mere deliverance.* You may have deliverance and no enlargement or development; or you may have both and grow. Seek development first; then deliverance, when it comes in God's own way

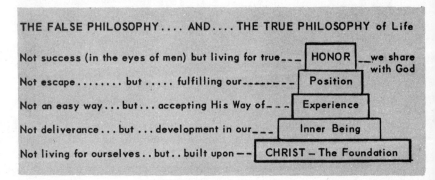

THE FALSE PHILOSOPHY.... AND.... THE TRUE PHILOSOPHY of Life

Not success (in the eyes of men) but living for true___ **HONOR** __we share with God

Not escape........ but ..... fulfilling our_____ **Position**

Not an easy way...but... accepting His Way of_ _ _ **Experience**

Not deliverance...but ...development in our___ **Inner Being**

Not living for ourselves.. but.. built upon — **CHRIST — The Foundation** and time, will be more meaningful. Learn to accept trouble and adversity as one of the most skillful and wonderful instruments in God's hand to develop character and accomplish real fruitfulness unto Him.

So we see that our foundation cannot long be a secret. We are constantly giving ourselves away in the purpose and goal for which we are living. In one short sentence we can picture the difference in foundations: "...them that honor me I will honor"—that is the true foundation; and "...they that despise me (and really live for themselves) I will esteem lightly"—that is the wrong foundation.

All of this would emphasize again how utterly important is our basic philosophy of life. It is quite generally acknowledged: until you have completely changed a man's philosophy you have really made no lasting change. It is like dealing with the mainspring or fundamental motive.

THE TRUE SOURCE OF HONOR

From whence cometh true honor? We must now see that honor is never something we should seek to receive apart from Christ. In the ultimate sense, true honor belongs to God and we only share it with Him. Consider the spotlight which is placed upon the king as he sits upon the throne. He is in the place of highest honor. Then he beckons to his faithful wife to join him at his side — and she steps into the light to *share* in his honor. How much greater is her honor as it is related to him than if she were merely some woman out on the streets. When the spotlight falls on her apart from her husband, she comes short of that higher honor.

So it will be with us. Any honor we may gain or seek apart from Him will only be empty by comparison. Indeed there is a most subtle kind of honor-seeking amongst men who do not know this. Making *our honor* the goal of life is to make our happiness depend upon others, and happiness should be something one cannot take away. Our real goal then should be HIS HONOR.

This being true, how much more meaningful are the words in Hebrews: "...he who hath builded the house hath MORE HONOR than the house" (Heb. 3:3). Even so, let us learn this great secret that we are but His house—and our greater honor can come only as we participate with the BUILDER.

Now let us take one more good look at the various levels of the house which the Lord is building. It is doubtful that the Psalmist had these levels in mind, yet surely he pictures the same truth in other words. So it is with truth: The one most significant characteristic of truth is that it blends everywhere.

In Psalm 112 we have a lovely description of the man whom God exalts to share His honor. To the pastor we started with, we might share these words of comfort and exhortation. Notice how appropriate these three phrases are:

> vs. 6 "...he shall not be moved..."
> vs. 7 "...his heart is fixed..."
> vs. 8 "...his heart is established..."

How does God work this kind of steadfastness in the heart of His servants? The pattern has already been clearly pictured before us. The life must first of all be cemented to THE FOUNDATION. (A) Thus we read: "Blessed is the man that reverences the Lord." This is foundational. (B) We read: "unto the upright..." which speaks of one who is attuned in his inner being. (C) "...there ariseth light..." This light is that he might "guide his affairs with discretion." That is, the truth brings about experience and wisdom. (D) Finally he is established in position: "he shall not be moved..." and we see why "his heart is fixed..."—for he is "trusting in the Lord."

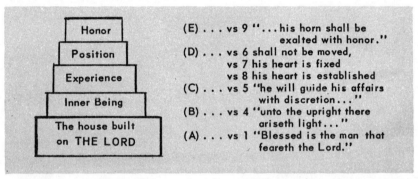

Honor	(E) ... vs 9 "...his horn shall be exalted with honor."
Position	(D) ... vs 6 shall not be moved, vs 7 his heart is fixed vs 8 his heart is established
Experience	(C) ... vs 5 "he will guide his affairs with discretion..."
Inner Being	(B) ... vs 4 "unto the upright there ariseth light..."
The house built on THE LORD	(A) ... vs 1 "Blessed is the man that feareth the Lord."

Now what is the final by-product from a life living in this steadfastness unto the Lord? Simply this: "...his horn shall be exalted with honor."

How well I remember watching the herd of cows on my grandfather's farm. It seemed to me (and has been verified by some farmers, I believe) that usually one cow became the "boss" in every herd. That cow would, so to speak, learn how to exercise her authority or lordship over the others. Do you know which cow seemed to gain that position? It was the one with the longest and sharpest horns. Perhaps this is the reason that throughout the Old Testament we have the horn as the picture of authority. When David or Saul were anointed with a "horn of oil" it meant they were given the official authority.

Now surely this is what the Psalmist means: "...his horn shall be exalted...." Those who have allowed God to build their personal house in His own way, can well expect He will not only give position, but the authority (horn) which goes with that exaltation. And what is more—the exaltation will not be empty; for it is "with honor."

Finally in this Psalm we must see how all of these levels are first an inward reality before they become an outward thing.

THE

ULTIMATE

SERVICE

DEVOTION OR SERVICE?

THE TESTING TIME OF
RELIGIOUS FOUNDATIONS

BY WHAT POWER DO
YOU MINISTER?

WHAT IS THE GOAL
OF OUR SERVICE?

IF YOU
WOULD SERVE.

Instrumental

Expressive

AFTER graduation from Bible college, Dave became assistant pastor in an evangelical church. For almost five years his days and evenings have been filled to the brim with Christian activities, leaving little time for his family and almost no time for reading, meditation and prayer. While he is not aware of it — for he has never known anything different — his ministry seems to lack depth; and despite all his constant busyness in what he sincerely believes is "the work of the Lord" his life does not have the fragrance or reality of one who lives close to the Lord Jesus. He is alive to opportunities for service, yet is missing life's great opportunity.

IN CONTRAST, Grandpa Wilson has been confined to his home for several years. His arthritic condition will not allow him to attend the church activities though he can enjoy the morning service via radio. For years the whole church has been conscious of something unusual in his life. It is that close intimate walk of fellowship with His Lord that has caused pastors, relatives and friends to seek his counsel. He seems always to have just the right word from the Lord to meet every need. Those visitors who came "to minister" left with an awareness that they had been ministered unto—for there was always a strange flowing of LIFE from his inner being.

WE MUST CONSIDER WHETHER OURS
IS MERE SERVICE OR TRUE DEVOTION

YOUNG DAVE and Grandpa Wilson differ greatly in their outlook on life's main purpose. The young assistant pastor feels that "by their fruits ye shall know them" and that soul-winning and service are the marks of sal-

95

vation and spirituality. Hence he feels that numerous meetings, activities and large numbers reached for the Lord are the measure of one's sacrifice, commitment and dedication to the Lord. He is a victim of our religious times: To him it seems that *doing* is more important than *being;* that spiritual zeal is the yardstick for measuring reality.

Grandpa Wilson has long ago embraced a different philosophy of life. He knows that to God our love is more important than our labor, and that it is worshippers, not workers, that God is seeking first of all. He comes from the old school who insisted with the Westminster catechism that "man's chief end is to glorify God and enjoy Him forever."

INSTRUMENTAL OR EXPRESSIVE – WHICH?

Now the issue we consider is not whether to serve the Lord or not, but what is the real nature of our service. It is true that God uses any thing as much as He can. He uses the flowers and trees to reflect His glory. As we behold their beauty and grandeur we cannot escape the all-glorious One who made them. However in man He has placed the faculty of will and mind which allow us to cooperate with Him. While lovely flowers may be instrumental in their service, it' is the will-factor which God has given to man that makes for an expressive service. The measure of His using us depends then, upon the relationship to Him which we allow. We may be used like the flowers—merely instrumental, but that is far below God's high calling for man. By His design we are capable of being expressive. Let us probe into all that really means.

We can see that it is possible for us to be like a flower or a cold tool in God's hand. As a tool He can use us "for His work," yet our relationship to Him is merely instrumental—like a lifeless instrument yielded in His hand. Is not this the kind of service the great majority know? God uses them—but! He longs for a much more intimate relationship in which He can manifest Himself through the total personality. This is no more passive submission, but rather an active participation. It is by such deliberate cooperation that every hue of His Being, every quality of His Person should be expressed through us. It would seem one·can quickly detect that responsiveness, intimacy, or sensitivity to Him which manifests whether we are merely instrumental or truly expressive.

One has described the difference this way: "Though Judas Iscariot lived with Jesus Christ and the eleven disciples for three years, he seems never to have developed an expressive relationship with any of his companions, nor with his Master. His connection to them was based only on a feature: he was the treasurer. If any of them collected money, they had to go to him with it: if they needed funds for a purchase, they had to see him. He interacted with them as treasurer, not as intimate or personal friend. This kind of outward, superficial, and feeling-neutral relationship, the sociologist calls *instrumental.*"

In instrumental relationships, people interact for one purpose—to accomplish an outward, objective goal, not simply to enrich each other in mutual fellowship. How often we have observed this kind of concern in soul-winning cause the unconverted to react against those who would offer help. He seems to sense inwardly that they are merely interested in him as a piece of merchandise to rescue from the burning. It is not because of personal desire or worth, but they have a command to obey, a ministry to perform—there is such coldness and impersonal pursuit when one is used simply as a mechanical instrumentality.

THIS WAS GOD'S BATTLE WITH JOB

Just yesterday a friend alerted me to Job's real problem. God wanted to use Job in an expressive way, but he was boastfully content to be merely instrumental. You know how often folk quote just part of a verse and often overlook the remaining part. It is common to glibbly quote: "All things work together for good" and miss "to them who love God, who are the called according to His purpose."

There is another verse we hear so often used in part, and as with the verse above, it takes on full and proper meaning only as we add the missing part. How often you hear folk quote with Job: "Though He slay me, yet will I trust in Him:..." And there they invariably stop. Nine out of ten you may ask cannot possibly finish this verse. Yet it is utterly incomplete in meaning without these further words: "but I will maintain mine own ways before Him" (Job 13:15).

This is the all important key in Job's crucible experience. He insisted upon maintaining "mine own ways before Him." It is almost as though he were saying: "No matter what happens to me—I'll be instrumental and trust God to use me, but I reserve the right to maintain *my own ways*—don't ask me to be expressive."

We rejoice, however, by the end of the book that God brought Job into such a rectification and turning of his captivity that He could fully express Himself through a broken but actively cooperating Job.　　✸

ONE HAS CONFIDED:

"I'm ashamed to admit—I'm about to faint in the ministry. I look at some men who are changing churches, as though another pulpit would make an improvement in their ministry (and that may be God's will for some), but I've tried several changes and after the newness is over, the problems are the same. Others are seeking more education and schooling as though that were their great need for more effectiveness. Still others are yearning for new experiences of power, of utterance and boldness, as though God ought to impart some endowment to make them successful in their service. Can you share a word of counsel for a weary heart?"

GOD WILL BE EXPRESSIVE
THROUGH YIELDED PERSONALITY

OFTEN THERE IS NO OTHER WAY! God must allow us to dry up, to faint, to cry out in frustration as we come to the end of our own ways. It is His way of turning us from a dependence upon our preaching, correct doctrine, methods, experiences or developed abilities.

Perhaps no better example can be given of the secret of a fruitful ministry than that discovered years ago by Mrs. Booth-Clibborn, better known as the Marechale of France. How did she hope to conquer in religion-ridden and infidel France? Listen to that frail little woman:

I saw that the bridge to France was—making the French people *believe* in me. That is what the Protestants do not understand. They preach the Bible, they write books, they offer tracks. But that does not do the work. "Curse your Bibles, your books, your tracts!" cry the French. I have seen thousands of Testaments given away to little purpose. I have seen them torn up to light cigars.... Only if Jesus is lifted up in flesh and blood will He today draw all men unto Him. And the conviction that took shape in my mind was that if I cannot *give* HIM I shall fail. France has not waited till now for religion, for preaching, for eloquence. Something more is needed.

"I that speak unto thee am He"—there is a sense in which the world is waiting for that today.... Christ's primary idea, His means of saving the world, is, after all, personality. The face, the character, the life of Jesus are to be seen in men and women....

These were the convictions with which I began the work in Paris. I said, "We will lay ourselves out for them; they shall know where we live; they can watch us day and night; they shall see what we do and judge us." And the wonderful thing of those first years in France and Switzerland was—*the flame*. We lighted it all along the line. Wherever we went, we brought the fire with us, we fanned it, we communicated it. We could not help doing so, because it was in us; that was what made us sufferers. The fire had to be burning in us day and night.... We all know what the fire is. It warms and it burns. It scorches the Pharisees and makes the cowards fly. But the poor, tempted, unhappy world knows by Whom it is kindled and says: "I know thee who thou art, the Holy One of God!"

That was what filled the halls at Havre and Rouen, Nimes and Bordeaux, Brussels and Liege. We personified Someone, and that was the attraction. I have not the insufferable conceit to suppose that it was anything in *me* that drew them. What am I? Dust and ashes. But if you have the fire, it draws, it melts; it consumes all selfishness; it makes you love as He loves; it gives you a heart of steel to yourself, and the tenderest of hearts to others; it gives you eyes to see what no one else sees, to hear what others have never given themselves the trouble to listen to. And men rush to you because you are what you are; you are as He was in the world; you have His sympathy, His Divine love, His Divine patience. Therefore He gives you the victory over the world; and what is money, what are houses, lands, anything—compared with that?

This was the one attraction. When I went to France, I said to Christ: "I in You and You in me!" And many a time in confronting single-handed a laughing, scoffing crowd, I have said, "You and I are enough for them. I won't fail You, and You won't fail me." That is something of which we have only touched the fringe. That is a truth almost hermetically sealed. It would be sacrilege, it would be desecration, it would be wrong, unfair, unjust if Divine power were given on any other terms than absolute self-abandonment. When I went to France, I said to Jesus, "I will suffer anything if You will give me the keys." And if I am asked what was the secret of our power in France, I answer: First, love; second, love; third, love. And if you ask how to get it, I answer: First, by sacrifice. Christ loves us passionately, and loves to be loved passionately.

Indeed, the Marechale had paid the supreme price. She sacrificed all that she might be clothed in the mystic whiteness of Christ. She had the anointed eye to see men lost—lost because they have never seen Christ personified.

Before you are quick to change places of ministry, to run off for more schooling, to grasp for some experience of power, you might give time to ponder this question honestly and patiently: Have I really, wholly, utterly, completely, unreservedly become a yielded personality through whom He might express Himself? None who have allowed Him this right, have ever failed or fainted. MAY GOD AWAKEN US TO THIS SIMPLE KEY!

★

CHECK YOUR ATTITUDE BEFORE YOU READ THIS NEXT ARTICLE:

I am convinced God has commanded us to witness to all and leave every one without an excuse, even if it means raming salvation verses down their throat. No medicine is really desirable though it is most necessary. While they may not like our bold presentation of the Word, nevertheless they will never forget what we have planted.

Like an insurance salesman I am wholly convinced that I have the only Eternal-Life Policy that can be offered. Because it will guarantee heaven, blessings, peace of mind and happiness to all who will receive it, I am convinced that no sane, sensible person can ever turn down such an offer when they understand what it will mean for them.

Because I have seen those who are unwise in their zeal, who lack knowledge in the ways of the Lord, I have almost slipped into another extreme. In my desire to be casual and natural in winning confidence I must admit I have too often become indifferent, even careless—and may even leave the impression with those around me that I am unconcerned about their spiritual condition.

Since my life has come wholly under the government of the Holy Spirit, God has given me a new kind of spiritual "touch" in helping others. There is a boldness of the Spirit which disarms and yet a sincerity which wins. There is a discernment of the Spirit which penetrates and also a tenderness of the Spirit which heals whatever it touches. I have recognized that God has not called me to put pressure on others, for He reserves that right. But He does want to be expressive through me and thus apply an indirect pressure as others see a living reality demonstrated.

100

Is it really of God,
or our own misguided zeal . . .

WHEN WE TRY TO "HARDSELL" THE GOSPEL?

SEVERAL YEARS AGO I copied a sentence into the flyleaf of my Bible and each time I ponder it God speaks anew to my heart:

The boldness of the flesh disgusts,
the boldness of the Spirit disarms.

We know there are those times when the Holy Spirit will clothe one, as He did Peter or Stephen, to boldly declare the truth of Christ even in the most adverse circumstances. The remarkable result from such a ministration of the Spirit is that the hearer is completely disarmed. No words can counter the 'Spirit's wisdom. Who could withstand such searching truth as Stephen gave? His hearers were cut to the heart; all they could do was gnash upon him and stone him to death.

But I am more concerned just now with the tendency of many *would-be-soul-winners* who seek to "hard-sell" the Gospel. Somewhere they have imbibed the attitude that unless they present a verbal witness to every one they encounter they are either ashamed of or failing the Lord. They have accepted the same high-pressure techniques often used in selling insurance or a car. Like any other commodity, they would (hard) sell the experience of salvation.

The tragic results of this kind of witness—however well-meaning—is manifest all about us. The boldness of the flesh has only produced disgust; people have come to resent those who deal in a cold, impersonal, mechanical way; they naturally react against impulsive or uncontrolled zeal which would operate upon them as a tool upon some machinery. Who has not experienced the tense silence, the coldness and the indifference? The moment you hold out a tract to another you are met with a heavy blanket of resistance. Someone before you has already conditioned that mind to resistance. Someone with fleshly zeal and little knowledge has already closed that mind. You are immediately classified along with all the other "religious crackpots" who have sought to barge into that life without any prayerful, or Spirit-wrought preparation. Someone has already rushed ahead of you and God, not realizing that the Lord never exhorted anyone to "ram salvation verses down your neighbor's throat irrespective of your relationship to him."

Here is the point at issue: *am I merely instrumental or truly expressive?* If to me people are mere merchandise to be captured for God, mere statistics to be added to my soul-winner's record, mere "brands to be plucked from the burning," then my approach and methods will be cold, calculated, mechanical and systematic. I will rush them through my little assembly-line of verses, present the plan and elicit the necessary response to salvation. Of course I am depending upon the Holy Spirit! If I do my part faithfully, then He will do His part. So I am working, and I hope He is working. But alas, we are not working together, for when I am determined in my own ways I can only be instrumental. God is waiting for that hour when He can work through me—when, out of a living relationship, there can be an expressive ministry that is truly effectual.

To illustrate God's way of being expressive through yielded lives, let us turn to Paul and Silas. Perhaps those with an imaginative mind are confident that Paul and Silas had already cornered the Philippian jailer with a bold witness as he locked them into the prison stocks. But I believe that this is reading into their actions something which is "out of character" with Paul's life and the divine method. It is most likely that word of the furor in the city against these two preachers of strange doctrine had already preceded them and closed the mind of the jailer. No hounding of the jailer with the gospel would avail. God must open his heart, even as He had the heart of Lydia. Thus we shall consider four conclusions:

1. *God has not intended for us to apply pressure on others: He will do that in His own way.* The great difference between man's way and God's way, is that He usually starts by allowing pressure upon His own soul-winner. So it was with Paul and Silas. We see them under pressure and difficulty. How will they react in the darkness of the midnight hour, all locked up in some prison of circumstances—almost ignored by the One they are declaring? The real pressure is upon *them*, not the jailer. This is God's way of demonstrating reality, of expressing His glorious sufficiency in the desperate hour.

2. *When God allows pressure upon us, and we respond unto Him, He can express reality through us which none can deny.* It was like a shaft of clear light when I heard J.W. Follette insist: "The word *witness* in Acts 1:8 is from the original *meritas* from which we have the word: martyr. This means that the power to witness which God designs to give us, as the Holy Spirit comes upon us, is not for more facility of speech, or for thunderous eloquence and boldness, but it is an inward power to be a martyr—expressive of reality even unto death. Stephen demonstrated this power when, with steadfastness and compassion he looked upon the glory of the Lord and wept for those who threw the stones. That day the pressure was upon Stephen, and the reality which flowed was irresistible. Was it the preaching that convinced Saul of Tarsus, or was it the expressiveness of love and forgiveness which sent its arrow to that persecutor's heart? We must surely admit that through such expressiveness of the Spirit others are not merely *taught* but they are helplessly *caught*.

3. *God does not cheapen the Gospel by using "hard-sell" methods.*
He uses His own vessels, often when they are most unconscious of it.
By an indirect method He awakens hungry hearts to recognize reality.
It was in the hour of their distress that Paul and Silas gave their
greatest witness to reality. They "prayed and sang praises unto God:
and the prisoners heard them" (Acts 16:25). This was the test! Could
they sing in the night, praise God even though they had been wrong-
fully locked up in the prison of circumstances? What do we do when the
pressure is upon us? Grumble or glorify God? Here was their opportunity to demonstrate that nothing can separate from the love of God,
neither tribulation, distress, persecution, famine, nakedness, peril or
sword. Nay, in all these things we are more than conquerors THROUGH
HIM. This is God's indirect way of "selling reality"—observers are
least aware that they are being "caught"—there is no wall of resistance.

4. *In His appointed time, God will turn the pressure; He will precipitate some "earthquake" to bring the needy to those who can share
life-reality.* Once this jailer has been "caught" by the reality in Paul
and Silas, it is the appointed time for God to change the pressure. He
alone knows when and how to send an earthquake into the jailer's life.
He knows what upheaval to use when His appointed time has come.
There is something quite remarkable about the awareness of the inner
man. Regardless of how hard and rebellious one may appear outwardly,
when the earthquake strikes in his life, he knows where to turn. True to
pattern, the distraught jailer knows where to flee for help. It is to
those who can sing in the midst of trial. Without any "hard-selling" or
pressure on their part, the jailer entered into life-reality. God had those
who were expressive.

It is not our service that our Lord most longs for, but ourselves.
When He has us absolutely under His control, then He will accomplish
an expressive service that will give Him the most satisfaction and joy.

> "I would not have the restless will
> That hurries to and fro,
> Seeking for some great thing to do,
> Or secret thing to know:
> I would be treated as a child,
> And guided where I go.
>
> "In service which Thy will appoints
> There are no bonds for me,
> For my inmost heart is taught 'the truth'
> That makes Thy children 'free';
> And a life of self-renouncing love
> Is a life of liberty."
>
> (B.M'Call Barbour)

ALL SPIRITUAL MINISTRY IS . . .

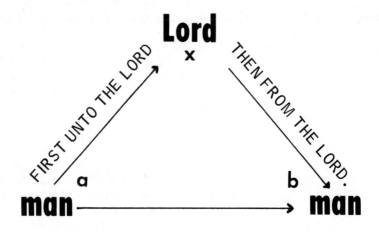

BY WHAT POWER DO YOU MINISTER?

ONCE IT HAPPENED LIKE THIS. You were invited to speak at a meeting where many noted celebrities would be in attendance. You sensed your inadequacy and trembled at your own weakness. Thus, utterly cast upon the Lord, you sought Him for help and experienced His special word and anointing for the message. In fact your excellence on the occasion so refreshed and astonished folk that you were immediately invited to appear before another group and give the same message.

However, the next week something happened—or should we say didn't happen. As you spoke the same words they lacked pungency, they failed to cut through the thick atmosphere and penetrate the hearts of those who listened. In your sense of struggle you tried a bit more power of personality or stress on dynamics and of course you got through. Many were appreciative, yet you left with an inward sense of emptiness. You felt sure your ministry was "in word only," not in power, in the Holy Ghost and in much assurance (1 Thess. 1:5). YOU WERE LIKE A GROUND WIRE WITHOUT THE HOT WIRE.

Or another time it happened like this: You were invited by a close friend to help his sister who was going through great mental stress and depression. Through the months you had faced many desperate situations and in your dependence upon God for direction you have been "much used" in bringing His liberation to others. But this time you find it impossible to fulfill your reputation. No insight or spiritual light is given. All your counsel falls like seed upon utterly dry ground. You leave with one hope. Maybe God has done something which is not yet evident, yet inwardly you groan under the strain and sense you were MERELY A GROUND WIRE WITHOUT THE HOT WIRE.

In the diagram we have pictured the two aspects of a ministry which flow like the current on two strands of wire. With the ground wire (A-B) we make contact with others. With the hot wire (A-X-B) we are attuned to the Lord, and His quickening falls upon the words we speak to make them life and reality. In the two incidents related above, there was an evident powerlessness. Any individual, when acting merely as a ground wire, senses no quickening or anointing upon the words which he speaks. What happens when the words are flat, empty and void of life? Are they not the same words which previously turned into a sharpened shaft with great piercing effect?

There is a hidden reason behind all the fainting and powerlessness in the ministry. What seems so utterly unpredictable to us, is however, really quite predictable when we have learned the secret the Apostle Paul reveals from his own ministry.

WHAT WAS THE SECRET IN NOT FAINTING?

In 2 Corinthians 4:1, Paul seems quite bold in announcing: "Therefore, seeing we have this ministry, as we have received mercy, *we faint not.*" In chapter three, verse five, Paul explains that this is a ministry of the Spirit. It is not merely letter, mere doctrine, mere words. If it were, he like so many today, would surely have fainted. But he had found a sufficiency that was no mere fancy—it was a reality. "Not that we are sufficient of ourselves . . . but our sufficiency is of God."

One can almost hear the Apostle say: "Once I knew only the ministry of the ground wire—I was merely contacting others in my own wisdom, strength; my words were empty and I was always fainting. Now I've discovered that all ministry is *first unto the Lord.* And since I have become primarily conscious of Him and His longing for each life I've realized all true ministry, then, comes *from the Lord.* He becomes as the hot wire."

Now many who know this in theory do not know it in working reality. Thus Paul goes on to consider those things which hinder this flow on the hot wire. We must hold one thing as basic. The Holy Spirit is a HOLY Spirit. He will not countenance the slightest infraction. He is easily grieved and the hot wire goes dead. So Paul urges: (2 Cor. 4:2)

We must "renounce the hidden things of dishonesty." How often it seems necessary and logical to allow a little dishonesty, but we must be alert to see how subtle and sapping this is, how deceptive and destructive. Dishonesty might happen like this: One morning in the midst of housecleaning, when the furniture is all out of place, the rugs outside for airing, you look out the window to see Mary Brown coming up the walk. You turn to your teen-age daughter with a sigh: "Oh, I wish she wouldn't come now—in the midst of all this mess." But as you greet her at the door you exclaim, "Oh! Mary—it is so nice to see you. Won't you come in?" Your teen-age daughter, for whom you have been greatly concerned and praying, registers in her inner attitude, "Mother doesn't always really tell the truth, nor does she mean what she says; she's not always completely honest."

Is the hot wire not working? You have been ready to faint? Perhaps you should cry out for an inward integrity and honesty of heart. David knew the importance when he acknowledged: "Behold, thou desirest truth in the inward parts." What sense of inward cleanness, inward confidence when you know there has been a continual yielding to His Spirit in every situation to be absolutely truthful no matter what the cost. Immediately you will find a new sincerity and can put away your acting ability.

We must "not walk in craftiness." Only recently a dear man, whom we have been counseling with, drove into our driveway and suggested: "You know, I'm greatly concerned for my son and his wife. Tomorrow they'll be at our house for supper. Why don't you just happen to drop in—say about 8 o'clock—without their knowing I've invited you." Then he proceeded to enlighten me as to their family difficulties, their weaknesses and problems. And he added, "Perhaps you could just happen to bring up this problem in your conversation."

Isn't that clever! I am supposed to just "happen along" while they are there. I am supposed to just "happen to discuss" those things as though the Lord were directing me to their need. This is just plain craftiness and God will not have part.

Fortunately, while in an earlier day I would have fallen into such a method of craftiness, I could now look into my friend's face and insist that God never honors nor does the Holy Spirit work with any one who uses crafty devices. As I look back on every occasion where I sought to fit into such a scheme, I cannot once recall having the help of the Holy Spirit. He simply will not be a part of our craftiness. It would seem there is much more dishonesty and craftiness among God's servants than we would care to admit, and it is the reason why the hot wire is not working.

We must not "handle the Word of God deceitfully," Have you ever been challenged by another to justify your position according to the Word? That is, when someone questioned your emphasis or doctrinal belief, you took your concordance and searched out all the references having to do with that subject. You found many that supported your conclusions, yet—alas, you found a couple which did not quite corroborate, in fact almost verified the other position. Did you with integrity use all the verses and explain that in honesty you must admit there were a couple of verses you did not fully understand? Or did you just ignore and pass over those references? While it is easy to "use the Word" to justify our position, when we handle it thus, we shall have "the letter" but not the anointing and inspiration which the Holy Spirit gives when we just "give forth the Word" and let Him make the application as He will.

I have been most amazed to see how the Lord utterly disarmed some cultist or one with an extreme interpretation as I took the Word (all of it) and opened it faithfully and honestly. Often to avoid handling it deceitfully I have even had to suggest that perhaps a single verse appeared to support their position, but I felt surely the whole body of Scripture must be allowed, not merely an isolated verse. And as I demonstrated that I had no private position to maintain but simply desired to stand with the Lord in His Word, there would often come a very peculiar and wonderful anointing which penetrated the heart to win far more arguments than my devious methods could ever have won. How blessed to have no position to defend—no trying to defend the Word itself. All we are called to do is handle the Word forthrightly, in simplicity and expect the One who controls the hot wire to quicken and breath life and meaning into mere words.

Finally, we have been showing how these hidden things—often overlooked—will thwart any true flowing on the hot wire. God cannot allow any hidden thing of dishonesty, any stopping to craftiness, or using the Word of God deceitfully by His servants. There are many who have claimed experiences of power, great crises of consecration, yet the deciding factor is this—is there a day by day sensitivity to God's holiness and integrity? Is there a continuous attunement *unto Him* so that there might be a flowing out *from Him?* This—and nothing else—determines the power by which we minister. The very moment the current ceases on the hot wire, we shall be forced to resort to the power of personality, of oratory, of pomp, of fame or of methods. Thus we miss the sufficiency of the Holy Spirit.   ★

I SENSED they had some pressing reason in inviting me home to dinner. As we finished eating, the husband began:

"Several years ago God seemed to work in a most unusual way in our farm community. Among us there were many folk converted. Then as we fellowshipped together and grew spiritually there were at least five families who determined to go all the way by entering fulltime service. Without going into details, in the course of time all five of us sold our farms (lovely Oregon bottom farms), pooled our resources and moved into the desert Southwest where we bought an abandoned town. There we started a mission for the Indians.

"At first enthusiasm ran high. The romance of our new venture carried us along. Then as we began to face some of the reverses and bitter realities of a life we were quite unprepared for, strife, bitterness, jealousy and frustration developed among the various families. One by one the families moved away to return to Oregon." Then, with a pause—and a sigh, he continued, "We were the last family to return."

For several days I had observed during the meetings that a cloud seemed to hang over this husband, wife and their teen-age daughters. Something was obviously wrong. Now I could understand their numbed and stoical response while God had been manifestly working in other lives.

As tears were coursing down this father's cheeks, he pleaded, "Where did we miss God's will? Can you fathom the disappointment and frustration among these five families who have lost most of their possessions, and now have no home to return to?"

With many varying details this story is being repeated throughout the country. Unnecessary heartache, suffering and confusion is thwarting the true calling and equipping of the Lord. Perhaps as never before we are now seeing . . . . .

THE TESTING TIME OF
RELIGIOUS FOUNDATIONS.

HERE WAS FAILURE! What had gone wrong? Surely no one is able to fully evaluate all the intricate factors in such an involvement. Without knowing the hidden motives, secret ambitions, self-will or unprepared and undisciplined lives, who among men is sufficient to understand unless God should give him a choice seat in His own viewpoint?

It would seem this tragic incident was a hey-day for the Enemy. The unsympathetic neighbors were quick to remind: "See, we told you it was a foolhardy venture." Relatives scolded: "You deserved to lose all, when you wouldn't listen to our counsel." Many of the church members seemed more smug and serenely set in their own lack of dedication and surrender. Even the more spiritual friends who should have been able to help, were too much like Job's vexing comforters.

Amid all the varied lessons which could be considered, there is just one basic thing we wish to emphasize. As I tried to show the family that afternoon, there can be little doubt that much of our system of religious service is built upon a wrong foundation: man beholds a need and attempts to meet it. Now, if we are merely interested in a humanitarian venture, that is different. The natural man can only rely upon his human sympathy to motivate him in this service.

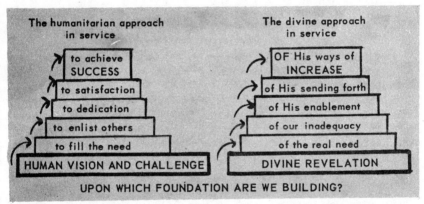

As we have pictured in the diagram, human vision and challenge is the foundation upon which most clubs, organizations, secret orders and lodges have built. Yes, even a great many churches have fallen to that level of humanitarian service. In building on the humanitarian approach of human vision and challenge, men move (1) to fill the need, (2) to enlist others, (3) to dedication, (4) to satisfaction, (5) to achieving SUCCESS. Let no one assume this is wrong. It is simply the natural man's approach and is wrong only because it becomes a substitute for the spiritual approach.

God's way is so different in the spiritual realm. Believers are called to a higher order of service in which the Holy Spirit is completely sovereign. He never allows us to see human need and then run off on our own to fill that need. Let us consider the plight of Moses when he did this:

"And it came to pass in those days, when Moses was grown, that he went out unto his brethren, and looked on their burdens..." (Exodus 2:11).

Immediately he is stirred to help one of his brethren who is being smitten by an Egyptian. "And he looked this way and that way, and when he saw that there was no man, he slew the Egyptian, and hid him in the sand." How exactly this describes what happens when man sees a need, accepts the challenge and tries to accomplish in his own strength. It is forty years later on the backside of the desert that Moses finds the proper foundation for spiritual service.

In God's own timing Moses receives a divine revelation (1) of the real need, (2) of his own inadequacy, (3) of God's enablement and preparation, (4) of His sending forth, and (5) of His ways of INCREASE. As we have pictured, the difference between true service and pseudo service is simply whether we move by divine revelation or by human vision and challenge. As it was with the family mentioned at the beginning, sometimes we only learn lessons through drastic means, but once we have discovered how imperative it is to build upon DIVINE REVE-LATION we shall never be moved by mere human challenge.

DOES THE NEED CONSTITUTE A CALL?

In considering the prophet Isaiah we have a perfect example of this divine order. We see how God builds upon REVELATION as the foundation for service.

FIRST: In chapter one, Isaiah receives a vision of Israel as a corporate man; from head to foot there are wounds, bruises and putrifying sores. God is acquainting His prophet with things as He sees them.

SECOND: In chapter six, a crisis develops. When King Uzziah dies, Isaiah the prophet is faced with a new king who is not favorable to his ministry. As the new king ascends to the throne it is the hour when Isaiah sees more than the need—he sees the Lord (6:1).

THIRD: As Isaiah sees the Lord he realizes the desperate need of his own life: "Woe is me! for I am undone; because I am a man of un-clean lips, . . . for mine eyes have seen the King . . . " (vs. 5).

FOURTH: In verses 6-7 we have God sending a divine purging and preparation for His servant.

FIFTH: It is because Isaiah's heart has become attuned to God's heart that he heard the voice of the Lord say, "Whom shall I send?" (vs. 8).

SIXTH: In verse 8 we hear Isaiah's response to the yearning heart of God: "Here am I; send me."

SEVENTH: In verse 9 we have the Divine sending forth, "Go and tell this people. . . . " Now, all of this divine order in Isaiah's commis-sioning would teach us several things. God never stops with just showing us the need, but will through some "king's dying" precipitate a means for our preparation and sending forth. It also would emphasize these things we cannot escape:

> If we have not been sent forth, it is most likely because we have never moved into a sharing of His heart and burden.
>
> If we have not moved in close to His heart, it is because we are still undone and unclean.
>
> If we have not been purged from our uncleanness, it is because we have never had a REVELATION of God Himself. And finally...
>
> If we are building upon any other foundation than a revelation of the Lord, we are building upon human vision and challenge.

We can rejoice that testing times will surely come to determine whether we are building upon HIS SURE FOUNDATION. ✷

PRINCIPLE   **In our service we are not merely to be faithful—but also triumphant. 2 Cor. 2:14**

"MY HEART HAS BEEN PAINED over the tragic troubles which bother the average minister. He is 'betwixt and between'—of all men most miserable. As somebody puts it, 'We suffer so much, but so seldom with Christ; we have done so much, and so little will remain; we have known Christ in part, and have so effectively barricaded our hearts against His mighty love, which surely He must yearn to give His disciples above all people.' All these things have brought upon you untold frets and worries. Like Saul. you are trying to save your kingdom. But you have actually suffered more miseries than the minister who has embraced the Cross. You have saved your life, but you have lost it, even in this world. The energy of the flesh not only spoils God's work; it spoils your own life and peace.

"Your trouble may be that you have been devoted to a cause instead of having the Cross as your sole inspiration, your one and only attraction. You have been ambitious to build your work. Shamefully you have made use of Jesus Christ. But as you contemplate cutting away these fleshly contrivances and

111

false ambitions, you become almost paralyzed with fear. You will be different! You will be reckoned a fool and a fanatic! Oh, the shame you may have to suffer as you humble yourself before your parishioners, your Sunday school, your class! Then think of the contempt you may suffer before your fellow-ministers or fellow-workers. I believe I know how to sympathize with you. But cheer up. Once you have been undone in the fires of God's furnace, you will come forth without the smell of your religious self!"

(L. E. Maxwell in BORN CRUCIFIED)

WHAT IS THE GOAL
OF OUR SERVICE?

N O ONE WILL HAVE moved very far in the stream of spiritual service before he is faced with certain tangent streams, little whirlpools or side eddies which would seek to divert his time, energy and money to that which is not truly in the divine stream. We have pictured four lesser goals which we are in danger of accepting:

There is the whirlpool of mere activity: Many zealous, young converts have fallen into this snare, never to get out. Someone has described such as "those fussy little people who are in a constant tremble of excitement—who think that the whole world depends upon their exertions—who wear themselves into a premature grave." Such are constantly seeking to suck others into their little whirlpool.

It is easy to deceive ourselves that *froth* means *fervor,* and that *work* is identical with *fruit.* Those who are thus caught and deceived are apt to deal with the less outwardly active and more spiritual minded of their brethren in a critical and cruel manner. Doubtless they have not meant to be unkind, yet they have misunderstood God's ways in working. Not infrequently such zealous activists can unwittingly become the tool of Satan to trouble the more sensitive and undiscerning souls. They can irritate and terrorize, burden and break down those who seek, in sincerity, simplicity, silence, and seeming slowness to faithfully serve their Lord. Indeed if God uses such at all, it is as saint-perfectors.

There is dedication to a "good" cause: Who has not groaned inwardly in watching some earnest soul become preoccupied with a good religious cause? Something has blurred the vision and one's energy is sidetracked and diverted to a mere tangent stream. It may be fighting

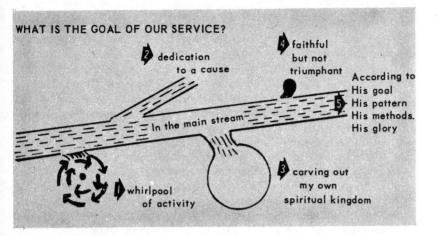

WHAT IS THE GOAL OF OUR SERVICE?

the liquor business, exposing Communism, promoting pensions, building an orphanage for children, raising funds for some religious enterprise, equipping a hospital or founding a skid-row mission. Now all of these have their proper place. But we must be careful lest we become occupied with a cause. While we are promoting a "work" we may be losing a spiritual ministry of touching needy lives and imparting life. God's primary method is *men touching men,* not machinery, organizations or religious causes. It is true that one can be in the midst of such machinery or promoting of causes, and yet have a ministry of life to those around him. It is in spite of—not because of—the religious cause. The danger is to unconsciously become so dedicated to the erection and perpetuation of machinery and causes as to lose a spiritual touch and anointing. Look at the by-ways in the religious world and you see men who have settled for a second best. They are too busy or preoccupied to realize their service is being diverted into a side-stream. No one can doubt their sacrificial dedication to a religious cause, yet all the while they are inwardly estranged from the LOVING PERSON they claim to devotedly serve.

3 *There is a carving out of our own spiritual kingdom:* Many dedicated children of God, while moving a great distance with their Lord, are nevertheless lacking in knowledge and discernment as to God's methods, pattern and goal in a truly spiritual service. While they are not wholly aware of it, they are carving out a little spiritual kingdom around themselves. It is not enough to insist that the work is for His glory and for the Body of Christ. If it is not according to divine pattern it is missing His goal. The question is: How much does this work depend upon them and their ministry? How much have they "built-up" the ministry of others so that they can become dispensable? What would happen if they stepped out? Are the people attached to them or the Lord? How much is the "work" related to the ultimate objective

113

which God is after? Have they allowed spiritual giants to eclipse all the brethren, allowed them to enlist others in a most refined kind of personal kingdom-building? Such spiritual giants become skilled as spiritual promoters, as diplomats, as strategists and as manipulators— using every device to build and perpetuate their own little kingdom.

Let no one assume we are writing out of bitterness or jealousy; nor because we delight in condemning others. We insist upon dealing with principles and not personalities. Nor do we infer that this present-day multiplicity of machinery and organization is not in any way contributing to the purpose of God. Rather, this is a plea to all God's servants to honestly bring their methods and motives under the scrutiny of His all-searching eye. In "His Light" we shall see whether we are building some self-styled kingdom for ourselves; whether we, with unbroken will or spirit, are perpetuating a sphere of ministry for ourselves simply because we cannot get along with others. We may avoid judgment of our service now, but in that hour of standing before the Bema, the judgment seat of Christ, we shall "see" whether our work was upon the proper foundation and whether our sacrifice and service was UNTO HIM and truly in mid-stream.

4 *There is a service that is faithful, yet not triumphant:* Many who have reached this point, who have discovered what it means to minister according to His pattern and goal find it easy to relax in the battle. They have become disheartened in the face of such bitter religious persecution and their "seeming to stand alone." The natural reaction is to find a little side-eddy where the pressure is not so severe, where one can console himself that really, we are not called to see our fruitfulness, but just be faithful. Then we shall hear that "well done, thou good and faithful servant." How tragic for a life to come this far, understand this much of the divine purpose and pattern, yet seek an easy way free from pressure. It is true, we are called to be faithful, but we are also to be triumphant in our faithfulness—not allowing an undertone of defeat. Hear the words of Paul: "Now thanks be unto God, which always causeth us to triumph in Christ... " (2 Cor. 2:14).

5 *Finally, there is a spiritual service that is in mid-stream:* When we have avoided the whirlpool of mere activity, when we have discerned the snare of dedicating ourselves to a mere cause, when we have rejected the ambition to carve out a little spiritual kingdom for ourselves, when we have determined with Paul to be triumphant in our faithful service—then we have fixed our eye upon His goal in spiritual service. We are moving in mid-stream. Then "we are unto God a sweet savour of Christ... " (2 Cor. 2:15).

In the coming journal we shall consider more fully what it means to serve according to His pattern, His methods, His power, His glory and His goal.   ★

If You Would Serve

On the hillsides in Kucheng District the most valuable trees are often marked with the owner's name. A common way of conveying water from the mountain springs down to the villages is in channels made of lengths of bamboo fitted one to the other.

A beautiful tree stood among scores of others on a lovely hillside, its stem dark and glossy, its beautiful feathery branches gently quivering in the evening breeze.

As we admired it we became conscious of a gentle rustling of the leaves, and a low murmur was distinctly heard: "You think me beautiful, you admire my tall stem and graceful branches, but I have nothing to boast of. All I have I owe to the loving care of my Master. It was He who planted me here in this very beautiful hill, where my roots, reaching down to and dwelling in hidden springs, and continually drinking of their life-giving water, receive nourishment, refreshment, beauty and strength for my whole being."

"Do you see those trees to one side, how miserable and parched they are? Their roots have not yet reached the living springs. Since I have found the hidden waters I have lacked nothing."

"You observe those characters on my stem? Look closely — they are cut into my very being. The cutting process was painful — I wondered at the time why I had to suffer — but it was my Master's own hand that used the knife, and when the work was fin-

ished, with a throb of unutterable joy, I recognized it was His own name He had cut on my stem. Then I knew beyond doubt that He loved and prized me, and wanted all the world to know I belonged to Him. I may well make it my boast that I have such a Master."

Even as the tree was telling us of its Master, we looked around, and lo! the Master Himself stood there. He was looking with love and longing on the tree, and in His hand He held a sharp axe.

"I have need of thee," He said. "Art thou willing to give thyself to Me?"

"Master," replied the tree, "I am all Thine own — but of what use can such as I be to Thee?"

"I need thee," said the Master, "to take My living water to some dry, parched places where there is none."

"But Master, how can I do this? I can dwell in thy living springs and imbibe their waters for my own nourishment. I can stretch up my arms to heaven, and drink in Thy refreshing showers, and grow strong and beautiful, and rejoice that strength and beauty alike are all from Thee, and proclaim to all what a good Master Thou art. But how can I give water to others? I but drink what suffices for my own food. What have I to give to others?"

The Master's voice grew wondrously tender as He answered, "I can use thee if thou art willing. I would fain cut thee down and lop off all thy branches, leaving thee naked and

(Continued on back cover)

Continued from back cover

bare, then I would take thee right away from this thy happy home among the other trees, and carry thee out alone on the far hillside where there will be none to whisper lovingly to thee—only grass and a tangled growth of briers and weeds. Yes, and I would still use the painful knife, for all those barriers within thy heart should be cut away one by one, till there is a free passage for my living water through thee."

"Thou wilt die, thou sayest; yea, my own tree, THOU wilt die, but MY Water of Life will flow freely and ceaselessly through thee. Thy beauty will be gone indeed. Henceforth, no one will look on thee and admire thy freshness and grace, but many, many will stoop and drink of the life-giving stream which will reach them so freely through thee. They may give no thought to thee it is true, but will they not bless thy Master who has given them His water through thee? Art thou willing for this, My tree?"

I held my breath to hear what the answer would be. "My Master, all I face deepened as He took what remained of the tree on His shoulders, and amid the sobbing of all its companions, bore it away, far, far over the mountains.

But the tree consented to all for the love of the Master, murmuring faintly, "My Master, where Thou wilt."

Arrived at a lonely and desolate place, the Master paused, and again His hand took a cruel-looking weapon with sharp pointed blade, and this time thrust it right into the very heart of the tree—for He would make a channel for His living waters, and only through the broken heart of the tree could they flow unhindered to the thirsty land.

Yet the tree repined not, but still whispered with breaking heart, "My Master, Thy will be done."

So the Master with the heart of love and the face of tenderest pity dealt the painful blows and spared not, and the keen-edged steel did its work unfalteringly till every barrier had been cut away, and the heart of the tree lay open from end to end, and the Master's heart was satisfied.

IF YOU WOULD SERVE . . . .   Read this parable of the Bamboo . . .

have and am is from Thee. If Thou indeed hast need of me, then I gladly and willingly give my life to Thee. If only through my dying Thou canst bring Thy living water to others, I consent to die. I am Thine own. Take and use me as Thou wilt, my Master."

And the Master's face grew still more tender, but He took the sharp axe and with repeated blows brought the beautiful tree to the ground. It rebelled not, but yielded to each stroke, saying softly, "My Master, as Thou wilt." And still the Master held the axe, and still He continued to strike till the stem was severed again, and the glory of the tree, its wondrous crown or featherly branches, was lost to it for ever.

Now indeed it was naked and bare —but the love-light in the Master's Then again He raised it and gently bore it, wounded and suffering, to where unnoticed till now, a spring of living water, clear as crystal, was bubbling up. There He laid it down— one end just within the healing waters. And the stream of life flowed in, right down the heart of the tree from end to end, along all the road made by the cruel wounds—a gentle current to go on flowing out, ever flowing, never ceasing, and the Master smiled and was satisfied.

Then the Master returned to His tree and lovingly asked, "My tree, dost thou now regret the loneliness and suffering? Was the price too dear —the price for giving the living water to the world?" And the tree replied, "My Master, no, a thousand times no!"—By B. E. Newcombe.

The ULTIMATES

THE

ULTIMATE

GIVING

WE MUST ALSO
LEARN TO RECEIVE!

THREE KINDS OF
GIVING

WHAT ARE THE LAWS
WHICH SHOULD GOVERN
OUR GIVING?

THIS PRIORITY
IN YOUR GIVING?

Have you discovered....

This

Priority

in your

Giving?

A young novitiate in one of the preaching orders of the middle ages was eager for the time when he might begin to preach. At last the superior said to him, "Come, we will preach today." Joyfully the young man set out with the superior. As they walked through the narrow streets of the town the superior gave a coin to a beggar, spoke a word of sympathy to a poor widow, and dried the tears of a weeping child. The little ones clung to the skirts of his robe as he passed, and their parents begged for his blessing. After a long walk, the two turned again toward the monastery. "But when are we going to preach?" asked the younger. "We have been preaching all the time," replied the elder.

How anxious we are to preach when our pulpit stands before the crowd; anxious to be "of service" when the applause of man is forthcoming, but how hard it is to single out that one "down-and-outer" at the well unless we can be sure she will tell all her friends what we have done for her. How we love to minister when it *ministers* to the man who "craves it the most."

As they continued walking back that day the elder again remarked: "You know, my son, long before we moved out to the people this morning there must have been an uttermost *giving of ourselves unto God.* Then what we give—whether our presence, our coins, our smile or our words—all will be freighted with His fragrance and have true meaning. Perhaps this is why the Apostle Paul tells us how the Macedonians *"first gave themselves unto God"* and then their love in their offering. Early tomorrow morning before we go out preaching let us be sure we have discovered this *priority* in our giving!"

AFTER A SERVICE one night a young man came to me with these words: "I wish God would give me this victory you have spoken about." I realized he had completely missed the whole point of my message. Suddenly it seemed the Holy Spirit directed me to say, "Look, God is no longer in the giving business; He is all through giving."

With a most startled look he replied, "But I don't understand how that can be." That moment it seemed utterly beyond his comprehension that God, the Father, had already given and was . . . .

NO LONGER IN
THE GIVING BUSINESS.

AS WE OPENED our Bibles I explained that the Father had already given His Son, the Lord Jesus, and in Him had given us all things. When one has already given all, there is nothing more to give. Then we turned to 2 Peter 1:3 and read: "According as His divine power hath given unto us all things..." I asked, "Does it say here that God will give, or that God should give, or that God has already given?"

He was quick to answer. "No, it says that He hath given—which means He already has."

Then in order to see *how* God had already given to us all things, we turned to Romans 8:32 where Paul writes; "He that spared not His own Son, but delivered Him up for us all, how shall He not with Him freely give us all things?" This verse clinched the fact that God had not spared His Son but already given Him—and thus with Him freely given— all things. If God had already given His best—His all—what else was there for Him to give! Next we read in Eph. 1:10 that the Father had purposed before time ever began that all things should finally be centered in His Son. It was not merely because man sinned, but even before sin entered, that the Father planned for all things to be accomplished in and through His Son. Of course the Son had been given as a means of redeeming us; but He has also been given as the means for realizing the Father's Eternal Purpose.

Suddenly it was as though a great light was breaking through. With a glowing countenance, I shall never forget, he announced, "I see it—what a breakthrough! After ten years of trying to get more things from God—mere peace, joy, blessing, assurance, even victory—I see that it is not God's way to give these. Glory! He gives us His lovely Son—and all these are in Him. Yes, God has already given—there is nothing more to give —is there?

As we sat down by the blackboard, I drew two diagrams for him: In the first diagram (A) we pictured man's usual conception of God's giving. Man assumes, in moving up the ascending stairway, that God first gives salvation, next answers prayers, then shares spiritual blessings, later offers victorious life, then provides an effective ministry and finally He rewards man with His personal presence as he reaches heaven. Thus in the end it seems man receives the ultimate of all God's giving.

MAN'S CONCEPTION of God's giving.   **A**

He will give....

heaven.

effective ministry,

victorious life,

spiritual blessings,

answer prayers

salvation,

He was quick to recognize man's warped conception which assumes that if man will give up, then God will give to man more and more. It goes like this: if man will give up his selfish ways, God will give salvation; if man will give time to pray, God will answer; if man will give up material things, God will give spiritual blessings in their place; if man will give up self, God will give victorious life; if man will give up his own ambitions, God will give him an effective ministry; and finally when man gives up this worldly abode, then God will give him a new home in heaven.

GOD'S INTENTION: **B**

He has already given us . . . .

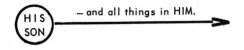

Now He waits for us to receive.

Then we drew the second diagram (B) which pictured God's intention in giving His Son. God does not start by giving man mere things. Folk may testify of receiving forgiveness, pardon, regeneration, salvation, peace, joy, blessing, victory—or a thousand good and important things— yet they manifest a lack of understanding in placing the emphasis on these things. God does not have various packages to dole out. What an amazing discovery, and yet how simple to comprehend! God starts at the very top of the stairway by giving us His lovely Son—nothing else, nothing more, nothing less. BUT IN HIM are wrapped up *all things* necessary for life and godliness.

By this time my new-found friend could sit no longer. Though he had been well versed in the Scriptures, suddenly verses came into new meaning and he began to exhort me. What a joy it was to hear him explain:

"I can see now why Paul said, 'But of Him are ye in Christ Jesus, who of God is made unto us wisdom, and righteousness, and sanctification and redemption' (1 Cor. 1:30)—yes, all we need has already been given in Him."

With abounding exuberance he continued, "And I can see why Paul insisted in Ephesians that the Father has already (past tense) 'blessed us with all spiritual blessings...in Christ Jesus.' " That night as he went out the door one could realize that a most radical change had taken place in his thinking. Only God could have wrought such a spiritual seeing, such a complete turning from seeking mere things to an appreciation of the glorious Son he had already received. It was quite meaningful when at last he announced: "I feel like a new man who is just beginning to discover what he already has in Christ. What I need most is to learn how to receive His fullness into my life, walk and ministry."

AT THE CLOSE of a morning service a sweet little four-year-old girl gleefully slipped to my side and dropped a package of pennies into my pocket. For several weeks, so I learned from her mother, she had been denying herself candy and gum that she might have this token of love to present to me. How happy this giving seemed to make her.

But it sent a pang to my own heart. When I thought of how easily I had often allowed pennies to slip through my hands, accepting this kind of love gift was not easy. In fact, I have many times discovered that if giving seems difficult—so is receiving.

WE MUST ALSO
LEARN TO RECEIVE

THERE IS AN IMMEASURABLE difference between *grasping* and *receiving*. Each grows out of a different kind of heart. Until we have been enlightened with a spiritual understanding it will seem like a real paradox when we insist that *receiving* is quite difficult, if not impossible, for the selfish or uncircumcised heart.

To receive graciously requires an inward work of His grace. Ever since the Fall man's whole inner life is bent on selfishly grasping and acquiring for himself. On the surface he may imagine that he is receiving, but until he has known the application of the Cross to the inner life: *the way of graciously receiving is impossible*—he can only grasp for more and more.

There is an old Chinese parable which illustrates this. "A certain man went to market with a string of seven coins. Seeing a beggar asking for alms, he gave the poor man six of them, and kept only one for himself. The beggar, however, instead of being thankful followed the good man and stole the seventh coin also." We may be amazed at the unthankfulness of the beggar, but what else could we expect from one until the life has been inwardly adjusted by divine grace?

THREE PHASES WE MUST UNDERSTAND

In learning to receive there are three phases we must understand. We shall call them the gateway, the pathway and the throne.

First, the gateway of repentance will unveil wondrous grace. As we have pictured, out of the heart of pride, blindness and selfishness issues the way of grasping; out of the heart of repentance, brokenness and dedication issues the way of receiving. How aptly are these two ways demonstrated in the Pharisee and the publican (Luke 18:10). In his attempt at praying, the Pharisee was grasping for attention; he was seeking approval or recommendation from God. In performing his religious observance he was trying to be worthy of receiving the grace of God. Yet in it all he was actually *grasping*. By contrast the publican manifested an inward brokenness in heart and in his spirit. In smiting his breast he reveals his sense of unworthiness and sinfulness before God. Just here we see the gateway: repentance. It is upon this guilty man who acknowledges his unworthiness to receive that God can pour His mercy and unveil His wondrous grace.

Consider the story of Charlotte Elliot. What a wretched night of conflict and tossing in despair before she finally acknowledged her true condition of sin and selfishness before God. It all began earlier that evening at the concert where she was singing. She had been confronted by an admirer who graciously sought to unmask her inner condition and self-righteousness before God. She rejected the help, and immediately was offended. But in fleeing home she could not run away from the piercing words that had been planted. Through the long night of sleepless tossing and wrestling she finally fell down before her Lord in repentance. Then the wondrous light of His grace broke into her darkened mind and she entered the gateway of life—receiving His forgiveness and mercy. No wonder she was able to pen these words we love to sing:

> Just as I am, and waiting not
> To rid my soul of one dark blot,
> To Thee whose blood can cleanse each spot,
> O Lamb of God, I come! I come!

Out of a broken heart it was possible for God to reveal that there was nothing she could do to recommend or prepare herself—only come as she was. So she wrote:

> Just as I am, Thou wilt receive,
> Wilt welcome, pardon, cleanse, relieve;
> Because Thy promise I believe,
> O Lamb of God, I come! I come!

Second, in the pathway of brokenness we shall discover the "riches of His grace." Indeed the first revelation of His grace accomplished by repentance is wondrous, but there must be a further unfolding. Through the pathway of brokenness we must now behold a still higher level: the riches of His grace.

A king once offered a subject a very magnificent present for some service rendered. "This is too much for me to receive," the man said. "But it is not too much for me to give," was the king's reply. He was rich and gave according to his ability to give.

THREE PHASES IN LEARNING TO RECEIVE

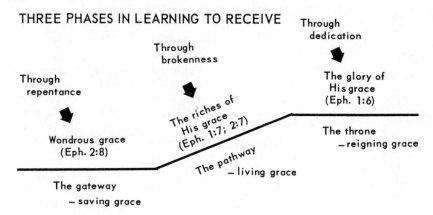

Through
dedication

Through
brokenness

Through
repentance

The glory of
His grace
(Eph. 1:6)

The riches of
His grace
(Eph. 1:7; 2:7)

The throne
— reigning grace

Wondrous grace
(Eph. 2:8)

The pathway
— living grace

The gateway
— saving grace

How deep are the roots of pride in a life—even in the life of a believer who is truly a subject of The King. It is just at this point He must lead us into the pathway of brokenness so we can behold HIM and His giving—not because of our worthiness—but because of His ability, because of the riches of His grace.

While we know the unregenerate man must come to God "just as he is" to receive (initial) saving grace, it is so easy for believers to slip into the subtle snare of trying to produce a worthiness to receive. It is just here the hidden roots of pride blind and God's only way is to take one into a deeper and deeper brokenness that He might fully unveil all that we have actually received in Christ. We are not only to enjoy *initial saving grace* but He wants us to learn how to experience *daily living grace.*

Third, as we are fully identified with Him at the throne of Grace, we can appropiate all things for the "glory of His grace." I believe we can see something quite distinctive between riches and glory. As a geologist I might discover the richness of a vein of precious ore. The more I penetrate into the composition and value of that vein, the more I uncover its true richness. But the glory of that ore comes only when it is refined and molded into something useable—such as a lampstand. Only as the ore fulfills its highest purpose can there be an unfolding of it's unique glory.

So it is with God's grace. We may discover it; we may even see its utmost richness, but until we behold its highest purpose, we have missed the ultimate glory of His giving (grace). This kind of glory we can only appreciate when we have moved into His viewpoint and by our dedication live identified with Him at the throne.

Let me illustrate with this incident. A very real crisis had come. A final payment on the new edition of books was due, so I bowed that morning to ask my Father for five hundred dollars to meet that bill. At the close of the morning Bible study a sweet little widow handed me an envelope. Without much thought I placed it in my pocket until a more convenient time to open and read the note. That evening as I prepared to go to church I detected the envelope and proceeded to open it. Here was a note with a check. At first glance I saw—$5.00—no, it was for fifty—oh—no, it was five hundred dollars—just the amount I had prayed for that morning!

I was stunned—and joyful. No one had ever done this before in more than ten years of meetings. But then as I reflected on her giving there was the strangest inward reaction. I wanted to rush to her home, and give it back. Only recently she had lost her husband; now she was laboring in a furniture factory to meet her needs—surely this was a great sacrifice—too much for her to make. In my moments of heart exercise I once again realized how difficult it was for me to receive graciously.

Then as I prayed, God seemed to open a whole new vista of experience which unveiled the glory of His grace. My difficulty was that I assumed she had given to me. I had not promoted this giving, but He had spoken directly to her heart—and she had given as unto Him. In a whole new way I saw what it meant to be identified with Him at the throne. Once we know we are one with Him in His dedication we can enjoy appropriating all things for Him. It is only when we imagine things are given to us that we become edgy about receiving. Indeed it is one thing to enjoy the riches of His giving, but still another to enjoy the glory of His giving.

There is an old story about a Scotsman, Lord Braco, who was very rich and miserly and who had great stores of gold and silver in his vaults. One day a farmer said to him: "I will give you a shilling if you will but let me see all your gold and silver." Braco consented. As the farmer gave the shilling he said, "Now I am as rich as you are. I have looked at your silver and gold, and that is all you can do with it."

Perhaps this would teach us that few of God's children even behold the riches of God's grace. They are hidden from view. Yet even those who behold the riches stop short of God's highest intention. Until there is a spending of those riches there can be no true fulfillment or purpose realized.

Perhaps this is what Paul is unfolding in Eph. 1:6 when he refers to the "glory of His grace." He tells us that it is the good pleasure of the Father to have a vast family of adopted sons (huiothesia) accepted in Christ Jesus, whom He can put on display before the whole universe. It is not merely His giving, nor the richness of His giving, but the ultimate purpose of His giving. This indeed is THE GLORY OF HIS GRACE.

Finally we can see there is much more in learning to receive than we had imagined. There is the gateway of repentance ,the pathway of brokenness and the throne for reigning and appropriating when we are fully dedicated to His purpose.

AN EVANGELIST CONFIDES: "Last night I was both embarrased and disgusted. It was the closing meeting of our series. The pastor had already plead for offerings in the morning and evening service to meet the weekly budget. Then he stood to further challenge the people to present a love offering to me, the evangelist. When he struck upon the idea of everyone marching forward to present their love gift upon the altar, I thought it was something new—but how embarrassing for many who could not give—or had already given under earlier pressure. I protested to him, but he assumed I was only pretending modestly, and insisted: 'Oh, they are accustomed to this.' "

Ever since that experience my heart has been aching for the Lord's sheep. I have suddenly realized how far we have drifted from God's intention in giving. It seems, today, that churches are either becoming more and more involved in mechanical methods of giving, or are forced to new ways of pressuring the sheep into giving. And what is so terrible is that once pressure methods are started, it requires increasing pressure. How sad that so many of God's sheep are being subjected each week to such pressure schemes. They are missing the joy and blessedness which should come as the Holy Spirit directs and develops them in spiritual sensitivity."

THREE KINDS OF GIVING

WE ARE QUITE AWARE THAT NOTHING is so "touchy" in the present-day religious realm, as an exposing of the object, methods and schemes in giving. But it has always been so. We recall that Jesus encountered the most violent reaction from the religionists of His day when on two occasions He entered the temple to deal with the money changers. Was it not so with Paul at Ephesus when it appeared that the silversmiths might lose their means of economic gain if the goddess Diana would be despised through his preaching?

Whether then, or now—one thing is quite evident. Religious authorities will "crucify again" anyone who dares to touch their source of finances. One has said: "Cut off the financial resources of any religious system and it will immediately die; cut off what seems to be the financial resources of a truly spiritual work—and it will make no difference, for it prospers by Spiritual life, not by material funds"

It is important that we distinguish between mechanical-giving, pressure-giving and Spirit-directed giving. We must recognize the foundation upon which each kind of giving rests; there are many things which seem to be "for God" which are really not "of God." We shall again see how the foundation we build upon determines everything.

What is mechanical giving? When giving is merely to fulfill obedience as a requirement of the law, when giving becomes simply a formal act which satisfies the conscience, when our weekly envelop falls into the offering plate only as a routine gesture unto the Lord—this is mechanical giving. Without realizing why, the great majority of believers seem to prefer the mechanical method of giving, for it shifts to someone else the responsibility of choosing who shall receive. And what is still far more serious is that many a zealous religious promoter has learned how to finance his dreams and visions with money given in this blind and mechanical way. Many religious institutions today are being perpetuated "for God" which have long since lost any spiritual value. Finally, let us say that any giving which neglects the exercise of our spirit, the vital concern of our heart and the intelligent understanding of our renewed mind is not Spirit-directed giving.

What is pressure-giving? When there is continued play on the emotions, when the human vision and challenge of the need is presented through soul dynamics, when increasing time is spent on developing new techniques and methods to stimulate giving, when promotion is paramount instead of prayerfully waiting before God to supply needs—

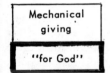

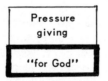

Mechanical giving	Pressure giving	Spirit-directed giving
"for God"	"for God"	"for God"
1. Obedience fulfills our only responsibility . . .	1. A great challenge of need, but out of mere human vision.	1. Through Divine unveiling of the real need . . .
2. The conscience is then satisfied.	2. The emotions are stirred.	2. The renewed mind is enlightened and the spirit exercised . . .
3. But often we are promoting a private kingdom for man's own glory.	3. Even though many projects are not according to God's pattern, there is a sincere sacrificing "for God."	3. By the Holy Spirit's prompting, such giving is really "of God" and brings glory to Him.

all these devices of men savor of pressure giving. Without realizing it many a congregation has become numbed—wholly insensitive to the Holy Spirit's prompting—because they have been subjected continuously to soulish pressure, to emotional appeals.

It has not become unusual for pastors to boast that their missionary budget has been increased year after year—until they have reached a figure which makes every competitor jealous. The end—being missions—justifies any means. So they pressure the people to sustain their vain ambition.

Many seem to have overlooked the loving concern of the Apostle Paul. He reminds the Philippians that he is not primarily interested in their gift—but is more concerned in the spiritual developement which giving will accomplish in their own life. "Not because I desire a gift: but I desire fruit that may abound to your account" (Phil. 4:17). We are sure that Paul encouraged the believers to systematic giving (1 Cor. 16:2) as well as intelligent giving (Rom. 12:1)—but he never stooped to pressure – giving or urged mechanical giving (2 Cor. 8:4).

In decrying this modern trend toward pressure giving, Lewis Sperry Chafer has written:* "Two widely separated methods of giving and of securing gifts are abroad in the Christian world. The one most commonly employed in is that of a direct appeal, often going so far as to suggest to the givers the amount they should give. The other method is that of depending only on the Spirit of God to direct the gifts in the case of every person, and then being willing to abide by the results of this confidence and trust."

He continues "...in presenting a cause, there is a difference between *information* and *solicitation*. All will agree that information is required, else no intelligent giving is possible, but the real problem centers around the question of solicitation. Many will recall the method employed for so many years by the late Dr. D. M. Stearns in his church in Germantown, Penna. He spared no pains or time to read the messages from the mission fields to his people, that they might be informed but so contrary to the usual practice, he would tell his people not to give unless to withhold their gifts would burden their souls. This was *information* without *solicitation*. The record is a matter of history that that church, probably beyond any other in a generation, from year to year with constant increase, led in sacrificial gifts to worldwide evangelization."

Recently we overhead a pastor sheepishly admit, "If I didn't apply any pressure on my people, I'm afraid I'd never succeed in any project I presented—in fact, the whole budget would cave in." What an admission!

What is Spirit-directed giving? When one has learned to distinguish between mere proposals of men and the divine pattern of the Lord for accomplishing His work, when one has learned to distinguish between

*From a tract: SPIRIT-DIRECTED GIVING – by L. S. Chafer

128

the emotional pull of the soul and the promptings of the Holy Spirit to his own spirit, when one is weary of helping men build their private religious kingdoms, which rise and fall with each personality, then he is truly ready to enter the pathway of Spirit-directed giving.

Again we quote from L. S. Chafer who explains two aspects of this kind of Spirit-directed giving: "First, the ecstatic joy of giving must be preserved. There is such a thing; 'for the Lord loveth a cheerful (hilarious) giver.' The ecstasy is nothing other than the inner consciousness that the gift is the out-working of the blessed will of God. There is a difference between being told by God and being told by men as to what and where we should give; and the giver, who is so dull of soul that he gives only under human pressure and responds only to strong emotional appeals, will know nothing of the true grace of giving.

"Second, in the stewardship of His children, God must direct the placing of gifts, else they cannot maintain a life of spiritual power and unbroken fellowship with Him. Why rob people of this blessing under the shortsighted impression that they must be coerced in their giving? Would that all pastors and evangelists might realize that the unbroken fellowship and the life of power are infinitely more to be prized than the financial gains! And would they might know that there is no trouble ever with the question of needed funds when the spiritual life is uninterrupted!"

THE TREND IN THIS PRESENT HOUR

Even the most casual observer will recognize that throughout the religious world today there is an increasing stress upon budgets, tithing, offering envelopes and income tax deductions. Without his consent, the discerning believer is being faced with pressure-giving on one hand or mechanical-giving on the other. Both our federal government and alas (too many) church governments are squeezing folk into a rigid pattern. But in taking the initiative away from the individual they are depriving God's child of that necessary sensitivity to the Holy Spirit's prompting. Organizations have hoped that this mechanical method will produce more giving, but we can be sure it will never equal that giving which is inspired by the Holy Spirit.

We can predict that difficult days are ahead for those of God's children who are determined to follow Spirit-directed giving. We were told recently, on good authority, that a church leader announced to hundreds of pastors under his jurisdiction that before the internal revenue will qualify any independent church in its giving, it must have the envelop system for at least five years. It is true that while the government is attempting to uncover religious racketeering and cheating among the unscrupulous, it is placing a bind upon Spirit-directed giving.

DR. GEORGE W. TRUETT tells of an occasion when he was raising money to dedicate a church building. The amount to be obtained was $6,500. After what he calls the slowest and most reluctant, most Christ-shaming effort to raise money he ever witnessed, they stopped at three thousand dollars.

After a long pause, Dr. Truett said, "What do you expect of me? I am your guest. I do not happen to have the other $3,500. What do you expect of me?" Then there arose a little woman back in the audience, plainly clad. "There was a surprising pathos in her voice," says Dr. Truett, as looking past me to the young man at the desk who was taking the names—her husband—she said: 'Charley, I have wondered if you would be willing for us to give our little cottage, just out of debt. We were offered $3,500 in cash for it yesterday. We were told we could get it at the bank any time if we chose to make the trade. Charley, I have wondered if you would be willing for us to give our little house to Christ that His house may be free. When we remember, Charley, that Christ gave His life for us, I wonder if we ought not to give this little house to Him.'

The fine fellow responded in the same spirit with a sob in his voice, saying: 'Jennie dear, I was thinking of the same thing.' Then looking up at me with his face covered with tears, he said, 'We'll give $3,500.'

Then there followed a scene beggaring all description. Silence reigned for a minute, and then men sobbed aloud. Gentle woman and men standing around the walls, who a dozen minutes before had shut their lips with scorn and contempt for a church halting and defeated, sobbed aloud, and almost in a moment provided the $3,500.

WHAT ARE THE LAWS
WHICH SHOULD GOVERN
OUR GIVING?

FROM THIS LOVELY STORY we can learn at least three laws which will be operative in our giving if we truly live to please the Lord and not ourselves. It seems evident from our story that Charley and Jennie had first given *themselves* wholly to the Lord, and now all that they had belonged to HIM. This is always God's pattern. They "...first gave their own selves to the Lord, and unto us by the will of God" (2 Cor. 8:5). As long as we reserve any right to ourselves, we still possess things as our own. And we will keep close records with God in our giving. In our possessing things we will be stingy, but when He possesses all, we shall learn to give sacrificially, immediately, single-heartedly and intelligently.

one Until we have given sacrificially, we cannot inspire others to give sacrificially. Surely this is the great bottleneck in giving. It is natural to want others to sacrifice, but not be willing ourselves. Without casting any reflection upon the servant of God who was raising the money in this incident, it does seem he could not break through the calloused hearts.

It seems there is a spiritual law that like begets like and sacrifice begets sacrifice. This uttermost sacrificial giving of Charley and his wife – an irresistible reality demonstrated – broke where a breaking seemed impossible. Again we see that brokenness begets brokenness. Out of their broken hearts flowed a stream which broke through every dam of resistance to flood dry and unbroken areas. Let us be careful lest we try to move others beyond our own experience of sacrifice.

two When we are spiritually sensitive our giving is always NOW. In our day (but it has always been so) it seems there is such a tendency to make promises to God. Next month we will be free from our present financial squeeze so we can give liberally. Yet strangely an unforseen emergency or opportunity arises and instead of getting out of the squeeze we only get more involved and in much deeper. Again we promise God that this next year we will get our affairs arranged so we can be free to give Him our time and talents. We mean well, but as next year dawns we find ourselves more involved in new and thrilling projects—even projects for God! And so year after year we imagine that it will be better "just around the corner." Thus it is that many have felt it quite sufficient to promise their future to God, yet reserve the present for themselves. They will even put God in their will. When they are dead and have no more need for security or wealth of course they intend for Him to have all.

I think we would be quite amazed just how much of the giving which we think is "now" has "future delivery" stamped upon it. If Charley were a typical "modern" we could imagine him answering Jennie, "Yes, my dear, I was thinking that the best way to help our church (and also ourselves) would be to will our property to the church and maybe the bank can hold the will as collateral against the mortgage." How easy it is to sidestep the Holy Spirit's direction and plan for future delivery instead of delivery now.

How often a church has been thrown into law courts attempting to gain through a will. Many times the best lawyers of the land cannot draw up a will that can withstand the onslaughts of friends and relatives. Let the believer move by the principle God has set forth in His Word. We are to live in the now: give while we live – as Charley and Jennie did. Instead of having folk get involved in bitter strife after we have gone, and even swear we were insane or that undue influence was brought to bear upon us, let us experience the joy of administering our affairs while we are here to see to them. Don't wait until our closing years, or some grasping relative will surely commit us and obtain legal rights over our property. Be sure of this—that believer who has learned to walk in spiritual sensitivity, has learned the joy of living in the NOW.

three In single-hearted giving our motive is only to please Him. We shall carefully guard against those hidden motives which lurk behind the surface motive. With Charlie and Jennie we are sure there was no desire to shame others, though they surely did; there was no intention of gaining the admiration of others; there was no hope to impress others with their superior spirituality; there was no intention of giving merely because it was an allowable income tax deduction. What crystal clear penetration of motive! It was as though everyone could look into these open simple hearts. With such singleness of heart she insisted: "When we remember, Charley, that Christ gave His life for us, I wonder if we ought not give this little house to Him."

But there is something else in this single-hearted possessing of things as though they belonged to Him. Having, does not to most people, appear as an opportunity for giving—they look upon giving as a loss because having is, in itself, so dear to them. In their shortsightedness they keep and keep and miss the joy of allowing all that belongs to God to flow through their hands.

DAVID MORKEN EXPLAINS ULTIMATE GIVING

WHEN OUR ELDEST SON, HUBERT, was a little fellow we were visiting at Balboa in southern California. One day we went out to look at the beautiful ships in the harbor, and Hubert seemed to want every one of them.

He would say with boyish excitement, "Oh, Daddy, wouldn't you like to have that one?" And he would point his chubby finger at a gleaming motor cruiser—or a sleek sailboat. As we approached a bigger more luxurious vessel that cost (so we learned) about $800,000 again Hubert said, "Daddy, wouldn't you like to have that one?"

"Hubert", I replied, "let me ask you a question. Suppose a man were to come to Daddy and say, 'Mr. Morken, I want to give you a choice between two things. You may become owner of all these ships in the harbor, and will add to them the *Queen Mary*, the *Queen Elizabeth*, and all the ships of the President lines. (Hubert was interested in ocean liners!) Furthermore, I will give you enough money to operate them all. That's the first choice. Or (and I pointed to Hubert) you may have this little boy.' Now which do you think Daddy would choose?"

Without a moment's hesitancy my son replied "Why, Daddy, I think you'd choose me."

He looked at me with his big brown eyes and said, "Because you love me."

I said, "Hubert, that is part of the reason." "What's the other part?" he asked.

"The other part is that you love me. If you owned that beautiful ship, we might have a lot of fun aboard it, but we could never love it, because wood and brass cannot receive love; nor can it give love. The ship could never love us. It has no ability to love anything."

I asked Hubert, "Do you know why you are worth more to God than all the stars in the heavens?"

"No," he said.

"Because," I explained, "God made the stars, and the biggest and brightest among them can be enjoyed by us all. They can be studied and measured by the scientists. God knows their names, but they cannot receive love, nor can they love God—or anyone else. But you can!"

WHAT IS ULTIMATE GIVING?

I N THIS LOVELY father-son relationship we have a clear unveiling of the ultimate issue in God's giving and in our giving. God gives to us all that really matters— HE GIVES HIMSELF. And we give to Him—OURSELVES.

If mere things could have satisfied Solomon, his vast wealth, his kingly glory and fame, and his amazing wisdom should have been enough. But he pronounced it all vanity of vanities. And if mere things could have satisfied the heart of God, He had a whole universe from which to draw. But there is in personality one thing which makes it utterly unique. By divine intention and design every personality is so constituted that it requires above all else the free response of fellowship, the flow of pure love and the mingling of spirit with Spirit. There is an indescribable "deep" within every breast that reaches out as an enormous vacumn to be filled. This deep within man reaches out to fellowship with other men. But there is also a "deep" within God which is ever calling out for fulfillment and satisfaction. The Psalmist must have described this: "Deep calleth unto deep as at the call of the fountainhead." It is God, the Fountainhead of all things who is calling out to fill our deep. It was this insight which caused Augustine to announce, "We are made for God and will never find rest until we rest in Him."

Down through the centuries it seems this union and communion has been the marked characteristic of those who experience ultimate giving. Meister Eckhardt said: "God can no more do without us than we can do without Him."

Watchman Nee (in THE NORMAL CHRISTIAN LIFE) describes how he went to visit the elderly George Cutting: "When I was ushered into the presence of this old saint of ninety-three years, he took my hand in his and in a quiet, deliberate way he said, 'Brother, do you know, I cannot do without Him? And do you know, He cannot do without me?' Though I was with him for over an hour, his great age and physical frailty made any sustained conversation impossible. But what remains in my memory of that interview was his frequent repetition of these two questions: 'Brother, do you know I cannot do without Him? And do you know, *He cannot do without me?*' "

DEAR LORD:

Forgive me for assuming,
  There is aught in life but Thee.
Forgive me for even breathing,
  When my source is not in Thee.
Forgive me for mere working,
  When it turns my heart from Thee.
Forgive me when my giving,
  Is less than all—to Thee.

THE

ULTIMATE

PREPARATION

PROFESSIONAL TRAINING AND
SPIRIT-WROUGHT PREPARATION.

THE DIFFERENCE BETWEEN THE
SHEDDING AND THE SPRINKLING
OF THE BLOOD.

THE DIVINE DISCIPLINE
THAT PREPARED ELIJAH!

TRAINING FAILS WHEN
CHARACTER IS NOT DEVELOPED

TRAINING FAILS WHEN

CHARACTER IS NOT DEVELOPED

HERE AT THE EDGE OF THE OZARKS where we live, many young workers are sent by home mission boards to help the unchurched and under-privileged. Because this work is often hard, demanding and unrewarding many fail. Most often the reason for their failure is simply a lack of character development—not a lack of formal scholastic training.

Scholastic accomplishment neither makes nor breaks a missionary. It is but one factor in the complex of influences which have formed the man himself. A man may be highly trained in medicine, in linguistics or in Bible knowledge, yet be an utter failure in his assigned task. Why? Because his training was deficient? Not at all, if you are speaking in a formal sense of skills acquired. It is the human factor, any mission director will tell you, that crumbles. Hands skilled to operate on sick bodies, tongue quick to frame strange sounds, mind stored with hundreds of Bible verses—all this can be true, but the man himself may still be untrained—lacking in character development.

Formal training can be a most subtle stumbling block to its own usefulness. In our human way of thinking, formal training carries with it some sort of prestige that feeds personal pride, so that in the field of his specialization a man is afraid to make a mistake lest he appear incompetent. The application of hard-earned skills and knowledge to new situations where mistakes in action and judgment may become obvious to others demands genuine humility and moral courage.

Often those with the highest grades in language courses, for example, when faced with another language where that particular skill will no longer serve, find that fear and pride paralyze their efforts. Such failure is not due to lack of ability or skill, but to the character of the individual. He has in fact failed to learn from and during his training the very thing that alone can now make it useful in application.

Essential training, then, should produce disciplined—self-disciplined, Spirit-disciplined men—who know how to exercise wise control over their time, appetites, passions, tongue, thoughts; men who have learned how to operate on a Spirit-directed system of priorities, on their own, away from the helpful stimulus of Christian fellowship and meetings, or in the midst of pressure toward mediocrity among many Christians. We can see why so much training has failed; it is not mere skills and knowledge attained but the *character produced* that is basic to the resilience and flexibility necessary to meet situations without cracking.

PRINCIPLE   When our natural training has taken the
place of spiritual preparation we have accepted
a deceptive substitute. 1 Timothy 1:12.

RECENTLY AT A CONFERENCE several folk felt led to drop this confidential word to me: "We hope you get to talk with Brother ————. You know he has left the ministry and is working part time (in a secular job). We can't understand, after all these years of training in our Bible school, why he seems to be floundering. There are churches who would call him, but he insists on waiting."

When the opportunity came to fellowship with this brother. I found (as is so often the case) that it was well meaning friends who did not understand God's working with him. The professional training which friends were looking at and the Spirit-wrought training which God was after are wholly different things. He was not guilty, as many are, of selling out for the materialistic gain which will allow ease, security, comfort and a standard of living to satisfy fleshly appetites. What others could not understand was the wonderful awakening God had wrought in him. He had "seen" the difference between...

PROFESSIONAL TRAINING AND
SPIRIT-WROUGHT PREPARATION.

GOD HAD HEARD THE CRY of this young man who refused to continue in the religious pattern of mere professional service. It was evident that for months the Lord had been teaching him on the backside of the desert. There in God's own private schoolroom he had been going through an emptying of man's ways and an instructing in the ways of the Lord. As he shared with me some of the precious lessons learned, I rejoiced in the insight which God had given. Truly, "The preparations of the heart in man...is from the Lord" (Prov. 16:1).

This is an hour of great religious shaking. Yet only those with an open heart before God are understanding the shaking. Many have cried, "Make me fruitful at any price, dear Lord," and then they have experienced the strange pathway of spiritual preparation which God has designed in answer to their prayer. What humiliation it has meant as God has sought to wean them away from the applause, approval and acceptance of even the closest friends and relatives, that they might walk wholly before Him and unto His pleasure.

I think one of the most difficult things to convey to young people and enthusiastic laborers is that God's way is to ask them to lay down (even) their religious training. Oh what death! What frustration! After all those years of specialized training in a seminary or Bible college—and then to lay it aside! What a disgrace it appears to the present day religious mentality! How confusing to be employed in some (secular) way when you are "trained" for Christian service!

Yet here is the deciding issue. There is such a difference between a Spirit-wrought ministry and a professional ministry. I must honestly say —in my limited evaluation—it seems that often the greatest and most effective spiritual work is being done by those who are not "in the (professional) ministry" as such. While it is true that hundreds who have left the professional ministry may have missed God's plan and purpose at this important junture, yet this is also the very juncture where many have entered into a new sphere of fruitfulness. Having "seen" God's way they could no longer "fit into the traditional pattern" of professional service. As they left the "professional ministry" to pass through death into resurrection, God could accomplish a spiritual preparation and develop a truly Spirit-wrought ministry.

History records the remarkable movement of God when men have ceased being mechanical and merely instrumental in their ministry. Consider David Brainered and his ministry among the Indians. Dying in his youth, one of his last prayers was "for the influences of the Divine Spirit to descend on ministers in a special manner." On his deathbed he said to his brother, "When ministers feel the special gracious influences of the Holy Spirit in their hearts, *it wonderfully assists them to come at the consciences of men, and, as it were, to handle them; whereas without these, whatever reason or oratory we may employ, we do but make use of stumps instead of hands.*"

What was the secret of Brainerd's ministry? We see him praying for days with strong crying and tears for the anointing of the Spirit to come upon him. And when he was heard, he could take hold of the hearts of those callous Indians, not with "stumps" of human reason and cold theology, but with the "invisible and irrestible fingers of the Spirit." Is not this the secret to Brainerd's amazing revival scenes among the Indians, when the very heavens seemed to drop conviction and conversion, prostrating the Indians all over the community? This was not the fruit of professional training, but rather the fruit of Spirit-wrought preparation.

It would seem from the testimony of the Apostle Paul that he had "put himself into the ministry." We know he was brought up at the feet of Gamaliel—trained according to the strict letter of the Jewish religion. Much has been made, perhaps too much, of the fact that Paul was from Tarsus, one of the top three university cities of the day. When presenting his academic and religious credentials, Paul always referred to his Jewish training, and in writing to the Philippians he insists that "...If any other man thinketh that he hath whereof he might trust in the flesh, I more: Circumcised the eighth day, of the stock of Israel, of the tribe of Benjamin, an Hebrew; as touching the law, a Pharisee; Concerning zeal, persecuting the church; touching the righteousness which is in the law, blameless. *But what things* were gain to me, those I counted loss for Christ" (Phil. 3:4-7). Paul lay down every last confidence in the flesh that he might "know resurrection power and life" not in theory only but in actual fact he "suffered the loss of all things."

In terms of his training and past life, Paul might naturally have felt that his ministry would be to the Jews, that Jerusalem was where God would now use him. Even after the revelation of God's will by Ananias, Paul returned to Jerusalem, apparently minded to stay there. When the Lord urged him to leave, he argued that his former anti-Christian activity there would give more weight to his witness. God was insistent: "Depart: for I will send thee far hence unto the Gentiles." The Lord had His own plans for Paul's life. Paul's background and training were not the deciding factors, although the Lord made ample use of both on many occasions.

In the light of this we can appreciate anew how God put Paul into that ministry He had chosen for him. "... I thank Christ Jesus our Lord, who hath enabled me, for that he counted me faithful, PUTTING ME INTO THE MINISTRY" (1 Tim. 1:12). Once a zealous Paul had *put himself into a professional ministry* but now the Lord was to prepare and put him into a vital ministry. Like Paul, many have run before they were sent, and now they languish under the accusation of people and the Enemy because they have "left the ministry which *they* had entered." They had missed the divine pattern. It is God alone who can select, enable and prove a Paul or Barnabus in the church of Antioch and in the appropriate time thrust them forth into a Spirit-wrought ministry.

Perhaps we are writing to one who has a pulpit, yet no anointed ministry of *life;* one who conducts a Sunday School class, yet has no heart passion for the needs of others; one who is a professor in a school, yet has no liberating reality in his own life by which to envision the students; one who is a missionary yet has no expressiveness of Christ which alone can break through the language and cultural barrier. May I say it kindly, yet frankly: there are so many today who have entered a professional ministry yet God has never been able to accomplish a Spirit-wrought preparation in them; hence He has not PUT THEM INTO HIS MINISTRY.

A BIBLE SCHOOL STUDENT testifies: "For years I emphasized only the death-side of consecration. I moved about with the smell and spirit of death upon me. Then in His goodness, God unveiled the life-side of consecration. Suddenly it became more than a doctrine—it became a living reality as I saw...

THE DIFFERENCE BETWEEN THE
SHEDDING AND THE SPRINKLING
OF THE BLOOD."

REFERRING TO THIS PASSAGE in chapter 8 of the book of Leviticus, it is important to note what happened at that particular point in the consecration of Aaron and his sons to the priesthood. The ram of consecration was brought; Aaron and his sons laid their hands upon it; and then it was slain, its blood was shed. That blood was then taken and put upon them at different points of their beings.

There we have two sides of consecration. The shedding of the blood is the death side, and the sprinkling of the blood is the life side. The blood poured out is the life poured out, delivered up, let go or taken away. Sprinkling is the making active and energetic of the ministry in a living power. When you recognize that, you understand what consecration is, and also the meaning of the laying on of hands, the act of identification with a life poured out, a life yielded up, a life let go, a life taken away unto death. In the act of sprinkling a new position is represented, implying that now there is no longer anything of the self life, but all is livingly of God, active by God, and unto God alone. That is consecration.

Chapter 17 of the Gospel by John is known to us familiarly as the High-Priestly prayer of the Lord Jesus. He is there, in effect, advancing to the altar in an act of consecration of Himself, in the behalf of His sons, whom He is seeking to bring to glory, that they may behold His glory, and that the glory which He had might be theirs. Here is undoubtedly that which is represented by Aaron and his sons. The High Priest is consecrating Himself, as He says, that they also may be consecrated. The rest of the prayer is a wonderful exposition of the inner meaning of this part of Leviticus 8. In the little while at our disposal we shall seek to understand it more clearly.

The whole man has come into the realm of consecration on both its sides; the death side, and the life side; the life poured out, and the life taken again; the life let go, and the life resumed, but on another basis; the whole man is involved, as represented by his ear, his hand, his foot. That has a simple and direct message to our hearts.

THE GOVERNMENT OF THE EAR

We begin with the ear: "... upon the tip of Aaron's right ear." That means that the Lord is to have supreme control of the ear, that we must come on to the ground where the ear is dead to every other controlling voice, every other governing suggestion, and is alive unto God, and unto God alone. It is quite clear that, in some way, the governing faculty of every life is the ear; not necessarily the outward organ, but that by which we listen to suggestions, that, as we say, to which we "give ear." The suggestions may arise from our own temperament and make-up; the constraining things in our life may be our natural inclination; the pull and the draw of our constitution; deep-seated ambitions, inclinations, interests, which are not cultivated nor acquired, but which are simply in us because we are made that way. To listen to these is to have our lives governed by our own interests. Or it may be other things, such as the suggestions, the desires, the ambitions of others for us; the call of the world; the call of human affections; consideration for the likes of others. Oh, how many things may come to us like the activity of a voice, to which, if we listen, we shall become slaves and servants, and the ear, and the life with it, become so governed.

This illustrative truth in Leviticus 8 says, definitely and emphatically, to you and to me, that that shedding, that slaying, was the slaying of our ear and our hearing in respect of all such voices, and that sprinkling meant that we now have an ear only for the Lord, and He is to have the controlling voice in our life. The right ear, as the right hand, is the place of honour and power so far as the hearing and the speaking are concerned. Then you and I, if we say that we are consecrated men and women, mean that we have brought the death of Christ to bear upon all the government and domination of voices which arise from any quarter save from the Lord Himself. We are not to consult the voice of our own interests, our own ambitions, our own inclinations, or the voice of anyone else's desires for us. We must have an ear only for the Lord. That is consecration.

It is a solemn and direct word for everyone, and perhaps especially for the younger men and women, whose lives are more open now to be governed by other considerations, because life lies before them. It may happily be that the sense of responsibility about life is uppermost; the feeling is that it might be disastrous to make a mistake, and along with it there is a strong ambition to succeed and not to have a wasted life. Herein is your law for life, and although the course of things may be strange, and the Lord's ways ofttimes perplexing, and you may be called upon in a very deep way to give ear to the exhortation addressed to us in the book of Proverbs, "trust in the Lord with all thine heart, and lean not unto thine own understanding," nevertheless, in the out-working, you will find that *God's* success has been achieved, and, after all, what matters more than that, or as much as that? The course may be very different from what you expected, or thought, or judged would be the reasonable way for your life, but that does not matter so long as God has been successful in your life, so long as your life has been a success from God's standpoint. This is the secret, an ear alive only unto Him, and dead to everything that comes from any quarter other than the Lord Himself.

Chapter 17 of John's Gospel is an exposition of that. "They are not of the world, even as I am not of the world." If we were of the world, we should take the judgments of the world for our lives; what the world would suggest to be the course of greatest success, prosperity, advantage. The spirit of the world does sometimes get into our own hearts and suggests to us that it would be fatal for us to take this course or that. To give heed to that voice is to become conformed to this age. "I beseech you therefore, brethren, by the mercies of God, to present your bodies a living sacrifice, holy, acceptable to God, which is your spiritual service": and from the outset the point of supreme government is the ear. The ear must be put under the blood, to be God's vehicle of government. It means that we must have a spiritual ear. As children of God we have, by reason of our new birth, a spiritual faculty of hearing, and we must take heed to develop it as the Lord would have us do.

It means that the ear must be a listening ear. Many people hear, and yet do not hear; they have ears and they hear, but yet they hear not, because they do not listen. The Lord says many things to us, and we do not hear what He is saying, although we know He is saying something. There must be a quiet place for the Lord in our lives. The enemy will fill our lives with the voices of other claims, and duties, and pressures, to make it impossible for us to have the harvest of the quiet ear for the Lord. That ear must be an ear that is growing in capacity. The child has an ear, and it hears, but it does not always understand what it hears. A babe hears sounds, and you notice the signs of the babe having heard a sound, but that babe does not understand the sound that it hears. As it grows, it begins to know the meaning of those sounds. In the same way there must be a spiritual ear, a consecrated ear, marked by the same features of growth and progress.

Then, further, this ear must be an obedient ear, so that hearing we obey. Thus God governs the life from the outset.

THE WORK OF OUR HANDS

Then we come to the thumb: "...and upon the thumb of his right hand..." The order is quite right, the ear first and the hand next. The Lord must have the place of honour and strength in the activities of our life, in the work of our life. Now this all sounds very elementary, but we must listen for the Lord's voice in it. The point is, that in whatever we are doing, or about to do, in all our service, there must be death to self; no self-serving, no world-serving, no serving for our own gratification, pleasure, advantage, honour, glory, position, exaltation, reputation. In the death of our Offering we died to all that, and now our hand in whatever it does—and it may have to work in this world's business, to do a multitude of uninteresting things of a very ordinary character—whatever activity of life it has to engage in, on the one side, our hand is to be dead to self, and, on the other side, to work with the Lord's interests in view. "Whatsoever thy hand findeth to do, do it with thy might..." (Ecclesiastes 9:10). You will remember how much the Apostle warned about service being done to men, as by men pleasers, and not as unto the Lord. He was speaking largely to the slave of those days. When the slave system obtained—and the slaves had to do many, many things that must have gone much against the grain—he said to them: Fulfil your service, not as unto those men who are your masters, but as unto the Lord. We must question ourselves as to why we are in any given place, or what it is that moves us to desire any particular place or work. What is the governing motive of our ambition for service? Before God we must be able to say that any personal or worldly consideration is dead, and that our service now is not only not a reluctant, nor resigned giving of ourselves to what we have to do, but a ready applying of ourselves to even difficult, hard, unpleasant and uninteresting things for the Lord's pleasure.

Do write this word in your heart, that the Lord will not, indeed cannot, exalt you and give you something else, something more fruitful, more profitable, more glorious for Himself, until in that least, that mean, that despised, that irksome, maybe even revolting place and work, you have rendered your service utterly as unto Him, even if it has meant a continual self-crucifixion. That is the way of promotion. This is the way in which we come into a position where the Lord gets more out of our lives than we imagine He is getting. There is a priestly ministry in doing that difficult and unpleasant thing as unto the Lord, but we do not see that we are priests at the time. The idea of being girded with a linen ephod, at the time when you are scrubbing floors and washing dishes, and other like things, is altogether remote from your imagination. Yet there is a testimony being borne which is effective, of which, maybe, you have no consciousness. It may come to light one day. Someone may say: I proved that Jesus Christ is a reality, simply by seeing the way in which you did what I knew you naturally hated doing; it was wholly distasteful to you, you had no heart for it, but you did it in such a way that it convinced me that Christ is a living reality. That is no imagination and sentiment, it is true to life. The Lord has His eye upon us.

THE DIRECTED WALK

Next we consider the toe. "...and upon the great toe of his right foot." That means that the Lord is to have the direction of our lives, that all our outgoings and our stayings are to be controlled alone by the Lord's interests. We are not always being bidden to go. Sometimes the going is a relief, it is staying which is so difficult. We are so eager to go, and yet often the Lord has a difficulty to get us to go in His way. However the case may be, it is a simple point, it is a direct word. Our going has been rendered dead to all but the Lord, and our staying also. Our life has been poured out, has been let go, has been taken away, that is, the life which is for ourselves, of ourselves. Life has been taken up on another level.

THE SUPREME EXAMPLE

Apply that to the great High Priest. Had He ever an ear for Himself or for the world? Had He not an ear for the Father alone? Trace His life through again. Satan came to Him in the wilderness, and began to speak. We do not know how this took place. We know that the Lord must have spoken of the matter secretly and confidentially to some, for no one had been with Him. He had been alone. We do not know whether Satan appeared in physical form, and spoke with an audible voice, but the probability is that it was not so, and that he wrought rather by inward suggestion, the strong bearing down upon the Lord Jesus of certain other considerations, every one of which was in His Own interest. There is no doubt whatever that Satan spoke to Him in some way, and He heard what Satan said, but His ear was crucified, and the power of that voice was paralyzed by His consecration to the Father. In effect He triumphed on this ground: I have no ear for you, My ear is for the Father alone!

Satan came in other forms, not always openly, but under cover. Thus a beloved disciple would sometimes serve him for a tool: "Be it far from thee, Lord: this shall never be unto thee" (Matt. 16:22). The Lord turned and said, "Get thee behind me, Satan"; He recognized that as the voice of self-consideration, self-preservation; He was dead to that; this way of the Cross was the Father's way for Him; He had an ear for Him only. And so it was, all the way through.

Was it true of His service? Did He for a moment seek His Own ends by His works, His Own glory by what He did? No! Even in tiredness and weariness and exhaustion, if there were interests of the Father to be served, He was alive to those interests, never consulting His Own glory, or His Own feelings; and I have no doubt that His feelings were sometimes those of acute suffering. We read of Him as "being wearied." We know what that is, and how in weariness we would not only sit on the well, but remain sitting on the well, even though some demand were being made upon us. If we are the Lord's, we must be governed by the Lord's interests, and brush aside all the rising suggestions of looking after ourselves. So it was with Him in all His goings. He submitted His goings or His staying to the Father. His brethren would argue that He should go up to the feast, but He does not yield to their persuasions and arguments. His one criterion is, What does the Father say about this? His mother entreats Him at the marriage in Cana, and says they have no wine. His unlooked for reply is, "What have I to do with thee?" In other words, What does the Father say about this? So His whole life was, on the one hand, dead to self, to the world, and, on the other hand, alive only to God. And what a fruitful life, what a God-satisfying life!

There is a oneness with Christ in consecration. "For their sakes I consecrate myself, that they themselves also may be consecrated in truth." "I beseech you therefore... present *your* bodies a living sacrifice, holy, acceptable to God, which is your spiritual worship...." That is our priesthood.

Will you listen to that word? Will you take that word to the Lord in prayer? Will you get down before Him with it? Perhaps it is a word to bring about an end to a struggle, a fight, a conflict; an end to restlessness, chafing, lack of peace, lack of joy. You may have been fretted, you may have been thinking of your life as being wasted, and you are all in a ferment. Are you reaching out for something? Are you being governed by your own conception of things, by what other people think of you, by what the world would do, or what others would do, if they were in your place? These are not the voices for you to heed. What does the Lord say? Wait upon that; rest in that. You may not understand, but be sure a life on this basis is going to be God's success. Do you want God's success? God may do something through you for which you are temperamentally, constitutionally, altogether unfit, and for your part you have thought that, because you are made in a certain way, that must govern your direction in life. Not at all! Come, then, let us get down before Him on this matter, to deal with consecration, if needs be, all anew. – T.A.S.

THE DIVINE DISCIPLINE

THAT PREPARED ELIJAH!

I N READING FIRST KINGS 17 we see that God is reacting to the low state of His own people, Israel. There is a rising up in Divine discontent to lay His hand upon an instrument for recovery.

So Elijah stands before us to represent such an instrument, and, in God's dealings with him, we see the ways and the principles by which a servant of the Lord is made an effectual servant, in relation to the purpose of God.

PRINCIPLE ONE: God is sovereign in His selection. How often you have heard someone remark: "Wouldn't it be wonderful if Mr. _____ would yield his life to God! What talents he could use for the Lord! What training God could use! He could touch so many in his sphere whom others cannot reach!" Yes, how sensible this sounds. Yet it is wholly natural reasoning to assume that God chooses to use us because of our natural influence, our abilities, our prestige or our personality.

The first thing related to any such instrument is the sovereignty of God. There is never any adequate, natural explanation for the choice and appointment by God of His servants. There may be things in the chosen instrument which will be turned to account, when they are wholly sanctified and brought under the government of God's Spirit, but when all has been said, we have to recognize that God's choice of His instruments is always a sovereign choice, and not because there is anything naturally in the instrument to warrant His choosing that instrument and selecting it from others. He acts sovereignly in choosing and appointing for His purpose. But, although that may be true, and although God may go beyond choosing and may endue that instrument with spiritual power, yet the instrument must be controlled and disciplined continually by the hand of God. Otherwise that servant of the Lord, or that instrument, will be found following in the direction of his own soul, following his own judgments, being influenced by his own feelings. The intent and motive may be very good, it may be very godly, but that does not dispense with the necessity of that instrument being continuously under the hand of God, for government and for discipline.

Article by T. A. Sparks from booklet: THE MINISTRY OF THE SPIRIT. Principles (printed in san-serif type) are inserted by the editor.

PRINCIPLE TWO: God's way is continuous discipline and direction. Enduement for service may come as an initial crisis, yet God intends for His servant to enjoy a step by step dependence upon Him.

That is what comes very clearly before us at the outset in the case of Elijah. There is no doubt about God's sovereign choice, and there is no question as to God having endued Elijah with Divine power. Nevertheless, we see him at every step under the hand of God, and those steps are all steps which are a disciplining of the man himself. God is dealing with His servant all the time, and bringing him, all the way along, under His hand, so that he never becomes something in himself, but has everything in the Lord, and only in the Lord. We make a great mistake if we think that it is enough to have the Divine thought as to Divine purpose, that is, to have the knowledge of what God desires to do. That knowledge of the thought of God is not sufficient. There has to be a dealing with us in relation to that Divine thought, and that dealing with us is usually in a way which is altogether beyond our understanding.

PRINCIPLE THREE: Often the most severe discipline is to cheerfully follow God's leading—especially when we cannot understand the exact purpose in His dealings. As they pressed through the crowd, the little daughter tightened her grip on her daddy's hand and smiled: "Daddy, I'm sure glad you can see where we're going; down here I can only feel the pressing of these people."

If God were dealing with us as sinners, that is, if He were dealing with us because of certain personal sins and personal faults, we could quite clearly understand that; but when He is dealing with us in relation to Divine purpose, as His servants, His dealings with us go far beyond our understanding. We are taken out into a realm where we do not understand what the Lord is doing with us, and why the Lord takes certain courses with us. We are out of our depth, we are altogether baffled, and we are compelled—that is, if we are going on with God—to believe that God knows what He is doing: we have just to move with Him according to whatever light we may have, and believe that these dealings with us, so far beyond our understanding, are somehow related to that purpose with which we are called, and that the explanation waits some distance ahead, and we will find it when we get there. God does not explain Himself when He takes a step with us. God never comes to a servant of His and says, "Now I am going to take you through a certain experience which will be of this particular character, and the reason for this is so-and-so." Without any intimation from the Lord we find ourselves in a difficult situation, which altogether confounds us, puts us beyond the power of explaining that experience, and

God takes us through without any explanation whatever until we are free, until the purpose for which that experience was given is reached, and then we have the explanation.

The point is, that even an instrument, sovereignly taken up by God in relation to His purpose, while knowing His main thought as to His purpose, still needs to be kept every moment, at every step, under God's hand, to be disciplined in relation to that thought

Elijah, great man as he was, outstanding in the history of God's movements, was brought to that very point where, although He knew that God had laid hold of him, and although he knew what God's intention was, he could not, by his own initiative and by his own energy, freely go on to fulfill his mission. He could not move more than one step at a time, and even so that step had to be definitely governed by God. He could only take that step under the Divine direction. You see it here in this chapter to begin with. He had to take just one step, and then the next, and that by Divine direction, nothing beyond that. The Lord does not turn even His greatest servants loose with an idea. He does not liberate His most mightily used instruments to take a free course, even though they may know what God is after.

> PRINCIPLE FOUR: There are those times in a nation, in a church or in an individual life when things are in a deadlock. To deal merely with the outward, earthly, visible or human is to touch the surface. The only answer is for a ministry of divine authority to get at the real hidden issues.

Some of the reasons for that are clear. Elijah's ministry was one of Divine authority. There were powers at work which were more than human powers. The case with Israel was not simply one of spiritual declension. It was not merely that the people had lost a measure of spiritual life and were on a lower level than they should be, so that they had to have a deepening of the spiritual life. That was not the position at all. Baal had a mighty footing in Israel, and the evil powers, the forces of darkness, were back of this state of things. The situation demanded more than merely spiritual help to Israel. Something more than a ministry of exhortation and of spiritual food, something more than a convention for the deepening of spiritual life was called for. A ministry of Divine authority was needed, to deal with a spiritual situation back of the condition in which the people were found. There were mightier forces at work than merely human faults and failings. The mighty power of Satan was there represented by Israel's state. Elijah, therefore, must needs fulfill a ministry of Divine authority, and the very first public utterance indicates that that is what his ministry was:

"As the Lord, the God of Israel, liveth, before whom I stand, there shall not be dew nor rain these years, but according to my word." (1 Kings 17:1).

There is a position, and there is an authority by reason of that position. James says that by Elijah's prayer the heavens were closed. That is going beyond the merely earthly, human situation. And again, by his prayer the heavens were opened. That is authority in heaven.

PRINCIPLE FIVE: God, it seems, has never launched His servant into a public ministry without first a secret preparation. Let no one who longs to be effectual in service, imagine that he can escape having a unique history with God.

Now that ministry of authority was born in secret preparation before it came out in public expression. The Apostle James tells us quite definitely that "Elijah was a man of like passions with us, and he prayed fervently (you have no mention of that in the historic record in the book of Kings) that it might not rain; and it rained not on the earth for three years and six months. And he prayed again; and the heaven gave rain. . . ."

There is a secret history with God. He came into his public ministry with abrupt announcement. He simply stood there upon the platform of the universe, as it were, and made his declaration. But that is not all. There is a secret history with God behind that. All such ministry of Divine authority has its beginning hidden from the public eye, has its roots in a secret history with God. That kind of ministry, born out from that secret history with God, needs very special government by God to preserve its safety, to safeguard it from all those forces which can destroy it, and that is why Elijah, having such a ministry, needed to be governed in every step by God. There must be no generalization of movement in his case, there must be specific movement, God dictating every step. So God preserves that authority as He produces it, that is, by a hidden life. Such a life and such a ministry must not be exposed, otherwise it will be destroyed.

PRINCIPLE SIX: Because God knows human weakness and the snares of the self-life, He must train His servant in the life of separation, detachment and cutting off.

So the Lord said to Elijah, "Get thee hence..." Hence? Where from? From this exposure, this publicity, this open place with all its dangers. "Get thee hence, and turn thee eastward, and hide thyself by the brook Cherith, that is before Jordan." Hide *thyself*. Geography may have little to do with it. What is here spiritually is "hide *thyself*." Cherith means separation or cutting off, and that is linked with Jordan. Cherith is a tributary of the Jordan. We know what Jordan stands for, the death of the self-life. In the major sense, the Lord's servants have been to Jordan; that is, the self-life has been set aside; but they have to keep near Jordan, and Jordan has to govern them at every step. The most paralyzing thing to a ministry of Divine authority is "thyself." It is, in other words, the strength of our own souls. Elijah was a strong-minded man, a strong-willed man, a man capable of very strong and drastic actions, of pouring out a great deal of his own soul-life with great heat, and the self-life of a servant of God is a great peril to the spirit. Paul makes it perfectly clear that, at an advanced point in his ministry and in his spiritual life, when God had entrusted him with visions and revelations unspeakable, which it was not lawful for a man to utter, the main and most immediate peril and menace to the ministry of that revelation was himself. "Lest I should be exalted above measure...." Then the self-life had not been eradicated from Paul! Paul was not clear of the peril of doing great damage to purely spiritual ministry, and God had to take a special precaution against the self-life of his own servant, not the sinful life in its old sense, but the self-life. "Lest *I* should be *exalted*..." I... exalted! What is that? That is the exaltation of the *ego,* the self. What dangers are in that "I," and how truly it stands in peril of getting into an exalted place, a place of power, a place of influence, a place of authority. It is in this sense that the Lord has to say, "Hide thyself"; 'get to the place of cutting off, of separation.'

This was so different from what you might expect. You see, here is a man, having had this deep, secret preparation with God in much prayer, who finds himself brought out in Divine authority to make a great announcement which represents a crisis in the purpose of God. You would expect that, from that point, he would go straight on from strength to strength, from place to place, would at once become a recognized authority, a recognized servant of God, and be very much before the public eye. But God would guard against any servant of His taking up a Divine purpose and a Divine commission in himself, taking it up in his own energy. That will destroy it, and there must be a hiding, a very real hiding. If a geographical hiding is God's way of getting a spiritual hiding, well, be it so. If God chooses to send us out of the realm of public life and ministry into some remote and hidden place, in order to take us away from the imminent peril of our becoming something, of our being taken up to be made something of, our going on in the strength of our own self-life, that is all well and good; but whether it be geographical or not, the word of the Lord to all His servants would always be, Hide *thyself!*

> PRINCIPLE SEVEN: In learning the life of complete mobility and adjustableness one discovers that, what seemed as a permanent course is often but another transitional phase. It is, indeed, a most glorious hour when we recognize that, in a certain sense, we are always in a new transition — it becomes an expected pathway.

Then you see, connected with that, as a part of it, the servant of the Lord must be found always in the place where he is pliable, where the Lord can get a ready and immediate response. The servant has no program, therefore there is nothing to upset. He has no set course, therefore the Lord has nothing to break. He is moving with God, or staying with God, just as the Lord directs. He must be mobile in the hands of the Lord, that is, capable of being moved at any time; in any way, without feeling that everything is being broken up and torn to pieces.

"Get thee hence... and hide thyself by the brook Cherith... and it came to pass... that the brook dried up." The Lord did not say that it would not dry up, and the fact that the Lord told Elijah to go to the brook Cherith did not mean that the Lord was going to preserve the brook forever. It was a step, and the Lord said, in effect: 'That is the next step. I do not promise you that you will stay there always. I am not saying that that is your last abiding place, and that you can settle down there for ever. That is your next step: go there and be ready for anything else that I want.'

This is a spiritual condition, of course. No one is going to take this literally. If we were to begin to apply this literally, as to our business here on earth, we might get into confusion; but we have to be ready in spirit for the Lord to do anything that He likes, and never to feel that there is any contradiction when the Lord, having directed us in one way, now directs us in another. It is a matter of being in the hands of the Lord, without a mind of our own made up, though the way be hidden from our own reasoning, from our own will, from our own feelings, hidden from all our soul-life, so that the Lord has a clear way with us.

> PRINCIPLE EIGHT: God must uncover any hidden dependence upon other sources—even those He has seemed to provide. A friend, who is a faith-missionary, rather inadvertently remarked: "We've discovered our finances are supplied in almost direct proportion to the number of letters we mail to our supporters." Then he reflected a moment and his face turned red. With no little embarrassment he continued, "I know that sounds like we are dependent upon our friends instead of the Lord — but!" Indeed it was the beginning of a new uncovering of a hidden dependency, he admitted in months that followed.

The brook dried up! Well, are you dependent on the brook? If so, you are in a state of utter confusion when the brook dries up. Are you dependent upon the Lord? Very well, let all the brooks dry up and it is quite all right. Dependence on the Lord is a governing and an abiding law of true spiritual power. Elijah has been spoken of and written of as the prophet of power. If that is true in any special way, he was very certainly the prophet of dependence.

That relationship to the Lord made it possible for the Lord to do other things, and to lead him on into new realms of revelation and experience. Oh, what a thing adjustableness is! If we are not adjustable, how we prevent the Lord from bringing us into His full revelation and purpose.

Those disciples of John the Baptist were adjustable, and because of that they came to know the Lord Jesus. You will remember those disciples of John who followed Jesus, and said, "Master, where dwellest thou?" He said, "Come and see." Now had they been fixed and settled, saying, 'We are John's disciples and we must stand by him; we must stay with John, and move with him; let Jesus have His Own disciples, but we stand by John,' they would have lost a great deal. But they were open and adjustable, and moved beyond John.

Those other disciples of John whom Paul found at Ephesus many years afterward, to whom he said, "Did ye receive the Holy Ghost when ye believed?" were adjustable. When they heard what Paul said, they were baptized into the Name of the Lord Jesus. They were ready to go on from John to Christ, and so they came into the greater fulness (Acts 19).

Unless we are adjustable we shall miss a great deal. Elijah was adjustable, and so God could lead him on. The Lord allowed the brook to dry up because He had something more for His servant to learn, and something more to do through him, and so He said, "Arise, get thee to Zarephath . . . I have commanded a widow woman there to sustain thee." He went to Zarephath, and was made a blessing by his obedience.

> PRINCIPLE NINE: The lesson we are helping others learn on their level, will also become a lesson we must learn on our level. We must be careful to remember that coming to a "no water" experience does not mean we are out of the will of God. It is quite probably the evidence that we are in the direct will of His developing stature within us.

Then he was brought by his new movement of obedience and faith into a new exercise, a new perplexity, a new trial; for the woman's son died. The woman was a widow with one son. The death of the son meant for her the loss of everything. It happened while Elijah was there, being looked after by this woman, and he was there in his obedience to the Lord. He had done this in obedience to the Lord, and now, in the line of obedience to, and of faith in, the Lord, the Lord allowed this catastrophe to come into the very home to which he had been sent. It clearly raised a big question in Elijah's heart. 'God sent me here, I know that! God raised me up and commissioned me, and in the course of the fulfilling of my commission He brought me into this situation!

152

"GOD DOES NOT WANT YOUR TRAINING

HE WANTS YOU!"

IN THE PAST FIFTEEN YEARS I have met scores of young people who have given their training to the Lord, yet reserved themselves for themselves! It is one of the most subtle snares in our training today. Musicians want to give their developed abilities to God. Mechanics, doctors, teachers, nurses, linguists, pilots and even preachers—all want to dedicate their training unto Him for His service. It just seems right and proper, so we have become accustomed to this procedure. Bible colleges and seminaries turn out graduates by the hundreds who are professionally trained for service. Yet amid all this, we have an inner hesitancy and a gnawing conviction: *something is wrong.*

There can be no doubt but that God is concerned with training. The question is this: WHAT KIND OF TRAINING? We must discover the difference between natural and spiritual preparation.

We read that Moses "was learned in all the wisdom of the Egyptians." Philo credited Moses with proficiency in arithmetic, geometry, poetry, music, philosophy, astrology and various branches of education. Officially recognized as the son of Pharaoh's daughter, learned in all the wisdom of the Egyptians, with the best education of his day, Moses had every right to dream his dreams of a great career in Egypt, in the field of his training. He could serve both his people and his God.

We know then what a momentous choice it was for Moses, when he "was come to years", to renounce his favored position as son of the Palace, with all the social pleasures, the political privileges of his set, and "the treasures in Egypt." If we could have our way with him, we would rush him into a new sphere of service for God. Or better still, we would rush him off to Bible school for some specialized training in Christian work.

But here is the snare! There is many a "Moses" who has just come from Bible school and is wholly trained in the religious methods of our day. He has passed the courses on HOW TO DO IT. How to promote a sucessful Sunday School. How to develop an adequate music program.

And having learned in homiletics how to preach, or in speech class how to hold the audience spell-bound, he is now ready to enter the ministry. But I wonder if this is not the very juncture where Moses stood? God would remind us that whatever our professional or formal training may be—He has a special course in spiritual preparation. Is Moses willing to enroll in the divine school of hard and humbling work, in solitude, adversity, danger, defeat, misunderstanding, slander and humilation? It is not surprising that the man who emerged from the wilderness schoolroom was a man of great meekness, faith and faithfulness, spiritual boldness and intimacy with God.

Moses must have known he was called as Israel's deliverer. Did he ever wonder about wasting his training as he minded Jethro's sheep in Midian? George M. Cowan has suggested:

"It was Moses the man, the product of all his training, that God used. Formal training seems to fade into the background as a matter of prime importance. Before God could use him, He had to break him—position, prestige, power, training: all had to go on the altar with life itself. Then God used him, including his training, in ways His own wisdom deemed best. Who else could have challenged the wise men of Egypt, explained and applied the God-given moral, social and practical laws to a people raised in Egypt, as did Moses? God used his training, but there is absolutely no hint that this was any part of God's argument in guiding Moses into a knowledge of, and willingness to do, His will. Moses had already turned his back on *all* before God used him and it."

This is God's way. He asks us to yield our training to Him, not to be used—but to go into death. Then out of that awful losing our natural abilities and (even) religious training, He brings us INTO LIFE. Thus He puts all our training into a totally new perspective

May the Spirit of revelation help us to see that God only wants US. Our training—religious and even spiritual—He takes into death that out of resurrection He might bring forth a totally new kind of Spirit-wrought development and thus a spiritual ministry and service unto God.

THE

ULTIMATE

PHILOSOPHY

BEWARE! LEST YOU
BE SPOILED!

WHICH ONE ARE YOU?

THE ULTIMATE PHILOSOPHY
IS IN CHRIST

CONSIDER THE CHARACTERS
IN THIS MODERN CONTROVERSY

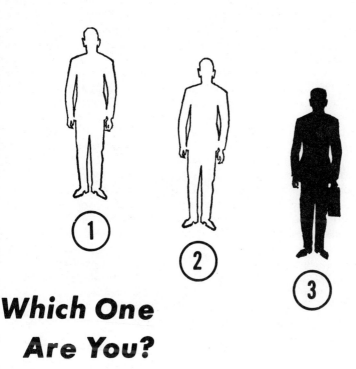

Which One
Are You?

EVERYONE IS BORN with a built-in mechanism which makes him a natural philosopher. Even from his earliest years man begins to seek to interpret the meaning and purpose, the relatedness and wholeness of life and this universe. The little boy who is forever bothering his mother with "why—why" is only expressing that first philosophical urge deep within which in manhood will cause him to search out the meaning and purpose of life. No matter how ruined man and his world may seem to be, and no matter how terrible man's despair may become, as long as he continues to be a man this built-in mechanism continues to tell him that life has a meaning. That, indeed, is one reason why man tends to rebel against himself. If he could without effort see what the meaning of life is, and if he could fulfill his ultimate purpose without trouble, he would never question the fact that life is well worth living. Or if he saw at once that life had no purpose and no meaning, the question would never arise. So we say that the vast majority of mankind are unwittingly philosophers. They have neither formally studied as philosophers, nor have they considered themselves to be such, yet they have been forced to develop a natural philosophy or way of life. If this is as far as you have progressed, *you are man number one.*

Then there are those who have followed this inner urge to discover meaning and wholeness in life. They have developed or are seeking to organize a formal system of thought to satisfy this inner quest. This small portion of mankind, often called the intellectuals, are usually the only ones who are labeled philosophers. One day Paul encountered this kind of philosophers on Mars Hill. These Athenians "spent their time in nothing else, but either to tell or to hear some new thing." When Paul confronted them with God as a living Person whom they *could know,* instead of an UNKNOWN GOD, immediately they showed their true color. They were simply in love with wisdom and knowledge itself. The word philo—meaning lover, and sophy—meaning wisdom, pretty well describes the subtle snare of philosophy. Like all pseudo philosophers, the Athenians were rejecting THE PERSON who alone could make all wisdom and knowledge complete.

One thing is quite evident: in spite of centuries of searching and formulating philosophies to explain life and its meaning, life is still an enigma to the natural and pseudo philosopher. If you are one who is still looking for the true meaning—hoping to grasp by your own searching, then *you are man number two.*

WHO IS THIS THIRD MAN? The Apostle Paul recognized this deep inner longing in man for answers, but he also knew that in a million years man could never by himself fit all the parts into a meaningful whole or understand the true purpose and goal of life and this universe. He insisted: what can never be *grasped* must be *given* by divine revelation. This revelation has already been given to us in the Person, Jesus Christ. Thus Paul wrote to the Corinthians: "Therefore none can boast in the presence of God. But from Him you exist in Christ Jesus, Who BROUGHT A PHILOSOPHY FROM GOD TO US . . ." (1 Cor. 1:30 Fenton Tr.).

In Paul we have the clearest example of one who refused to meet the Athenians or Corinthians on a philosophical basis. What a stumbling block to their pride and love of wisdom that he refused to stoop to using enticing words of man's wisdom but simply preached and emphasized Jesus Christ and Him crucified. As we shall see in the following pages, there are very few who have ever become *this third man*—one who so lives in Christ that He has become the very source, the center and circumference of life. The whole of Christendom would assume it has this divine philosophy in Christ. We shall see how this is not true.

A COLLEGE STUDENT TESTIFIES:

"It took quite a shock to awaken me! For months it seemed everywhere I turned—even in many 'Christian homes—I was finding books and records on *how to be successful, or how to achieve your goals, how to use the basic laws of the universe,* or *how to become rich.*

As I read and listened, these explosive new ideas seemed so helpful and inspiring. Like other people, I thought I could fit and adjust them into my Christian life and be a more effective Christian. The more I read and listened, the more I was captivated by the physcology and philosophy presented by men who seem to have mastered these laws. And I am sure ' iere were many things which helped me in my personality and outlook.

Then God answered my longing heart and showed me what was wrong! These ways for achieving goals, success, fame, prosperity, riches—were all good. They were even built upon Scripture and the principles in the Bible! But here was the snare: I was beginning to accept "another way." In developing these inner soul-powers I was using a *"way which seemeth right"*, but I was missing Him who is to be THE WAY for me.

What a glorious dawning has come! I have finally realized what is involved in the two trees in the Garden. In eating of the *tree of life* Adam was to become utterly dependent upon God for everything. Now when we receive Christ, He is to become our very Life, our Truth, our WAY—our everything.

Alas, there are too many who have accepted Him, yet they have not realized what it means for Him to be their very LIFE. They are still living *by* (that is) eating of the *tree of knowledge.* Thus in being independent of God, they actually are dependent upon knowledge—and it becomes their *way of achieving.*

I thought I was a spiritual Christian fulfilling God's will, but I really only wanted God to unveil His will so I could go out and do it for Him. That was just my trouble, I was even using the Bible as a *book of ways* for accomplishing God's work. I thought I was dependent upon Him, but actually I was always moving out in my own soul-energies to work for Him. It was *for* Him, but I was doing it.

At last I have seen what it means for HIM to live, to move, to will, to realize His WAY through me. What simplicity! What rest! What a discovery! Just to enjoy living in Him. Now in a whole new way the words I speak, the places I go, the whole of my life has its source in HIM—it is all *of* Him.

YOU CAN ACHIEVE YOUR GOAL IN LIFE   Order this dynamic LP record and discover the principles which have helped thousands of people become more successful.

In this record you have a sure-fire method for gaining prestige, wealth and fame. Listen to . . . . . describe the step by step formula that helped him turn $100 into a $35 million fortune.

Here in modern recorded form are the 13 proven steps to personal riches. These practical, money-making ideas, principles and methods will change your outlook and mold your thinking.

. . . . . famous author and psychologist presents ten proven ways you can overcome failure and discouragement. Your continued happiness depends on how well you learn to use these basic principles.

BEWARE! LEST YOU BE SPOILED!

IN THIS ISSUE of the journal we are taking a bold step, yet a most necessary one to expose the subtle snares of human philosophy and psychology. With gentleness, honesty and straightforwardness we must warn God's children to beware lest they be deceived and spoiled by a system of metaphysics which is presently invading and captivating many minds. While the world exploits its goods in a boastful manner, there are even servants of the Lord who have, we hope unwittingly, developed a like refined and Christianized approach for the church.

Reading material on most every bookstand is slanted to exploit the desire in men to achieve, to be successful, to be prosperous, to influence people, to be popular and to have magnetic personalities. The late A. W. Tozer warned: "This mania to succeed is a good thing perverted. The desire to fulfill the purpose for which we were created is of course a gift from God, but sin has twisted this impulse about and turned it into a selfish lust for first place and top honors. By this lust the whole world of mankind is driven as by a demon, and there is no escape."

It cannot be denied that scores and hundreds have read and practiced these laws of personality and become a success. Even careless, defeated

Christians have found their attitudes and habits revolutionized! By listening to these success records and reading books, they have become positive in their outlook. Through knowledge about their own makeup and personality they have become winsome and personable. Often what they thought was the offense of the Cross was discovered to be simply the offensiveness of their own disagreeable personality. Others have discovered what seemed to be the secret formula of happiness. Indeed these basic laws will work wonders for anyone who will use them. But... there is something wrong! What is it...?

From the very beginning, when Adam turned to his own way, God's great controversy with man has been over his insistence on being independent of God. God has uniquely designed man as a container to receive and express Himself. This means God will come into man to be his very LIFE—occupying, willing and fulfilling His purpose through him.

Like Adam, modern man has determined to develop his own soul-powers so he can fulfill his own way, his own goals and designs. Now too often we have assumed that these goals are always bad, evil or debauching. On the contrary, they are very often religious, philanthropic—really good. But they are objectives which the *natural man* is seeking to realize through his *own efforts*, his *own powers*.

To the undiscerning individual, the knowledge gained from the tree of knowledge we have pictured may be good, helpful and even give a real boost to successful living. That is exactly what the tree of knowledge has always been: good, but it is a substitute, a way for us to excel on our own without God.

Consider how this was the real issue when Satan tempted our Lord in the wilderness.Though a perfect man, our Lord had a soul and body just as you and I. It was possible for Him to act *from the soul,* that is, from Himself. Satan tempted Him to satisfy His essential needs by turning stones to bread; to secure immediate respect for His ministry by appearing miraculously in the temple court; to assume without delay the world dominion destined for Him. Perhaps you are inclined to wonder why he tempted Him to do such strange things.

You might feel that Satan should have tempted Jesus to sin in a more flagrant or outright manner. But he did not; he knew better. He only said: *"If thou art the Son of God,* command that these stones become bread." The subtle implication was this: If You are the Son of God You must do something to prove it. Here is a challenge. Some will certainly raise a question as to whether Your claim is real or not. Why do You not settle the matter finally now by coming out and proving it?

The whole object of Satan was to get the Lord to act FOR HIMSELF, that is, from the soul. But the Lord Jesus absolutely repudiated such action by the stand He took.

In the Garden, Adam acted *from himself* and *for himself—*all apart from God, and this was the whole tragedy of Adam.

RECENTLY during a morning Bible session the director of the YMCA where we were meeting, slipped into the service. Though I did not at that time know him, I recognized that he was immediately enthused and seemed to be receptive to the laws and principles I was explaining. I learned later that he had been presenting some of the very same principles to the men and boys in his Y membership. For almost an hour his was undoubtedly the most enthusiastic face in the audience. I knew he was being carried along by the "Christian philosophy" I was sharing. But I also felt sure he did not, then, realize I was setting forth the false "tree of knowledge" that I might contrast it with God's provision of Christ as our "tree of life." It was only as I proceeded to show how all of these laws and principles, which seemed so good, could become the most deceptive substitute that a noticeable change came in his expression.

Through the years I have watched this same initial enthusiasm in others. Men are always eager to learn the *ways for successful living*, but they are not usually interested in THE WAY which God has given. They will embrace a philosophy of life but not THE LORD JESUS as the Person who becomes our LIFE. Even when preachers present from the Bible the ideals, principles, ethics and laws for full and successful living,—there will be an amazing acceptance as long as Jesus Christ and His Lordship are by-passed or ignored. HE becomes the crucial issue! The very moment the conscience and heart are confronted with His rightful claim to govern the life, a strange wall of resistance develops. Men will rejoice in receiving more and more knowledge, laws, principles, and patterns for successful living, but they will studiously avoid THE ONE, whom God has given, who alone can implement and operate these laws in real fruitfulness. It is true men will make some progress in using these principles on their own, but only for a brief period. God has so designed everything that it will only function as Christ becomes all and all in life.

That noon as this director invited me to have lunch with him I found myself in a most enlightening situation. I guess I had never before realized that a religious man could have "another Jesus"—one who merely demonstrated these principles and laws in successful living. I also realized this man had "another Bible". By that I mean he used the Bible merely as a book of knowledge wherein were hidden principles necessary for solving life's problems. Perhaps our fellowship together helped him to see that Jesus Christ was God's answer, but I know I was helped to see, as I had not seen before, that . . . . .

THE BIBLE IS SO OFTEN
IMPROPERLY USED

WHEN SATAN SLIPPED into the garden to turn Adam and Eve aside, he could not accomplish his design without the help of something that was seemingly very good, necessary and important. We know that God wanted Adam to live from *the tree of life*, a tree which actually represented God, Himself, as all that was necessary for accomplishing life's true goal and purpose. But Satan was there enticing man to accept knowledge, not as God would impart it from Himself, but as it could be received through this "other tree"—the tree of knowledge.

Let me emphasize just how good and how deceptive this offer still is today. We might paraphrase it in this word picture: In my minds eye I can almost see Satan holding out the Bible and saying, "Here, let me show you the underlying principles of life; in this Book you will uncover the hidden patterns for successful living; let me help you search out the deep purposes and meaning of life."

How strange this sounds to us! We can hardly imagine that Satan would suggest a substitute way—that of using the Bible differently than God intended. Yet he is actually holding out the Bible as the "tree of knowledge" for fallen man to use in running his own life and realizing his own pursuits. We must hasten to say, just here, that God has never intended for His children to use the Bible thus; rather He has purposed that through His Word He might reveal Himself in Jesus Christ. It is by revelation that the written pages are to become THE LIVING WORD and thus truly become the "tree of Life" by which we live spiritually. So it is God who uses the Bible to speak forth "bread by which we are to live." It is true the natural man will *use* it as natural bread, but God intends that the Spirit quicken it into "living Bread."

Without realizing it there are, perhaps, hundreds of psychologists and philosophers who are using the Bible wholly as a book of basic principles. Without the illumination of the Spirit it is mere natural bread. And we fear there are even pastors and Christian workers who have fallen into this same snare: they would use the Scriptures for presenting Christian philosophy, principles, laws. They feed the mind natural bread, but they have not honored the Holy Spirit nor allowed Him to use His Word to reveal Jesus Christ as the Spiritual Bread who alone can meet the need.

As we have pictured in the diagram, the spiritually enlightened will not *use* the Bible but rather allow God to use His Book for revealing Jesus Christ as ALL THAT ONE NEEDS. Basically the question is this: Does God want to give us wisdom, knowledge, peace, comfort or joy? No, God actually does not want us to seek for nor does He want to give us any of these. He designs only to give us HIS SON and in Him all things are freely shared. It is true that down through the centuries and even today, many wearing natural blinds have turned to the Bible as a book of comfort, instruction, wisdom and peace. But if they received anything spiritual, it was the Spirit imparting Christ to them. Anything else was merely a feeding upon natural bread which may have had its own helpful effect.

In the diagram we have pictured how the natural mind will use the Bible as a source of knowledge. All across our land there are many who are boldly proclaiming that all their principles, methods, practices for successful living are found in or based upon the Scriptures. They will unashamedly insist that the laws for achieving honor, fame, riches and peace of mind are from this wonderful Book. There are countless thousands who have never bowed their knee to the continuing Lordship of Jesus Christ, thus allowing Him to become their daily Bread—the sustaining source of all wisdom and knowledge. What is even more alarming is that today among God's own children there are those who have fallen into this very snare: they are using the principles and patterns they have discovered in the Bible as the means for achieving their own "noble" ends.

It must be acknowledged that natural men have always enjoyed *using the Bible* for their comfort, strength and guidance. To them it may seem quite shocking to imply that their Bible is merely a source book. They see nothing wrong in using this Book for the unveiling of principles, the unveiling of patterns, the unveiling of the hidden purposes of life. All of this, they are sure, will help them *to be more like Christ*. And, as we

WHAT IS THE BIBLE TO US?

So we can live
more like Christ

...unveiling the
purpose of life
...unveiling the
patterns for living
...unveiling the
principles for successful
living

THE BIBLE.... used as a
source of knowledge

"the tree of knowledge"

Christ lives His
LIFE in us.

Christ unveils Himself
as the purpose of life.

Christ unfolds Himself
as the pattern for living

Christ reveals Himself
as the Principle for living

THE BIBLE...becomes a
revelation of HIM.

"the tree of Life"

have pictured they have built upon a wrong foundation. We are not to be *like* Him, but rather to allow Him to *live* His life in us.

May God apply the spiritual eye-salve to help us discern between that which is merely the *tree of knowledge* and that which is *the tree of life*. The great battle of the ages has never changed. It still centers in man's accepting that which is seemingly good, necessary and important as a substitute for accepting God Himself—in Christ. It is alarming that multitudes of believers are deluded in living from "another source" than God. Many who have not discerned how they are living from the "tree of knowledge" are blindly dedicated to promoting principles, patterns and purposes which seem so good—even seem spiritual! Yet they have missed the proper foundation. If they are not living by a revelation, that is, living by a *spiritual seeing* as their source and dynamic, they are plodding on by the impetus of knowledge. The songwriter was making this distinction when he said: "Beyond the sacred page I see Thee, Lord." How many get stalled on the sacred page. They do not meet Him, or find Him as the Living Revelation in those pages. All they receive is cold knowledge, life-less words. Jesus warned the religionists of His day: Ye... "Search the scriptures; for in them ye think ye have eternal life: and they are they which testify of me. And ye will not come to me, that ye might have LIFE" (John 5:39-40).

Now to be sure, there are hundreds in our fundamental churches who loudly proclaim that Christ is all we need, that He is completely sufficient, that Christ is our only center and circumference. These have become very proper slogans. But perhaps many have only learned these nice phrases and echo them as a parrot would. It seems quite evident that the real significance of *Christ as our all* has not dawned, for in the very next breath they launch into extensive methods, means and programs for accomplishing the work of God; immediately they start to search out patterns and principles for doing things—all of which are simply good religious substitutes for HIM. What a blessed hour of revelation to our hearts when we quite *using* things and allow Him to *use us;* when we cease looking for methods and allow Him to become the method in us; when we stop preaching knowledge and allow Him to display knowledge through us. Only then have we truly learned to reject all that issues from the "substitute tree" to find our all in the LIVING TREE.

Finally, we conclude that blinded man may improperly use the Bible but all he receives is knowledge; yet, when God is allowed by His Spirit to breath upon the Bible and use it first to quicken and then reveal Himself in Christ—men receive LIFE. The tree of knowledge and the tree of LIFE are so different! Would it seem too much to insist that God the Father is very explicit in His desire that we see only HIS SON as our sufficiency? As we shall consider in the following pages, if we miss the Father's LIVING REVELATION in His Son, we have missed all that really matters.

EVER LEARNING, YET MISSING THE TRUTH!

IN OUR LEARNING we can search the vast universe and its structure, we can grasp more and more about the things in the universe, but we can do nothing more important than learn to know God in a full and living participation. Down through the centuries the yearning pursuit of most every believer has been to really know God in a full-knowledge.

But it is interesting to observe that religious men, as well as many believers, have settled for something less than this experiencing Him in reality or participation in Him. They have been stalled in some outer circle and missed the innermost circle. In the diagrams we have pictured man's way of searching for this innermost reality (a to e); and then we have pictured God's WAY of taking us through the Cross to a position in Christ. From this new position of participating in Him we can through a full-knowledge come to appreciate the Person, the purpose, the ways

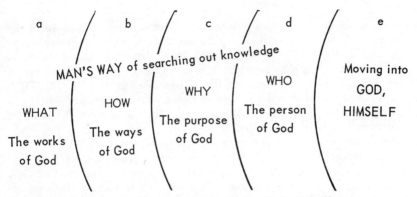

| a | b | c | d | e |

MAN'S WAY of searching out knowledge

WHAT

The works
of God

HOW

The ways
of God

WHY

The purpose
of God

WHO

The person
of God

**Moving into
GOD,
HIMSELF**

and the works of God. First we shall see man's futile efforts to move in to the inner circle (a to e); then we shall see God's provision for our living in Him and beholding all things new.

It might surprise us if we dared consider just how few of God's children have acturaly pressed into that inner circle of a living participation in Christ. While it is true every believer has experienced a spiritual birth from above, yet many have stopped short of appropriating God as their very fullness of Life—stopped far short of a living participation in HIM. Let us consider some of these outer circles where many get stalled:

a Have you ever met one who seemed completely absorbed in the *works* of God? All that really interested him was a deeper study and evaluation of God's miraculous works or His glorious handiwork. It is quite normal to stand in awe and wonderment at God's majestic creation; (in beholding all the glory and marvel of His design one can easily sense that he knows the One who made it all). While it is true God does speak through His creation and miracles, to stop with His works is to stop far short of knowing Him. This was the complaint of the Psalmist when he wrote that God could only make "known His acts unto the children of Israel." Their rebellion and unbelief hindered them from passing beyond this outer circle into a fuller knowledge. Those who will not accept the visible creation as the index finger pointing to the reality of the invisible God, will never move one step further in knowing HIM.

b Have you ever met individuals who became engrossed in searching out the *ways of God?* The Psalmist explains how much better it was for Moses than for the children of Israel. God "made known His *ways* unto Moses, His *acts* unto the children of Israel." How great a privilege it was for Moses to move behind the curtain of creation and behold the spiritual laws and principles which govern all God's works! One who has enjoyed the WHAT will surely appreciate the HOW even more. Once our eyes have become adjusted, we can see that God's ways are written so clearly into the fabric of things, yet the requirement is still the same if we would move into the next circle: God requires an honest and believing heart or we shall see no more. It is just here that so many stumble. Many with a scientific mind become engrossed in the *ways of God* and for a whole life-time accumulate more and more knowledge of His ways, His principles and laws. Are these the individuals Paul groans over when he says: "... ever learning (more and more knowledge) yet never able to come to the full-knowledge of THE TRUTH." Are the demands of complete honesty too great? To proceed further in knowing Him requires our rejoicing in all His ways—even rejoicing in those ways which seem to put us in a strait.

C Have you ever observed the philosophic mind which is continually asking why? Why? It is indeed necessary that we press beyond the *works* and the *ways of God* to understand the *purposes of God*. Why does He do things as He does? Could it be this was the deep yearning of the shepherd boy, David, as he gazed into the starry heavens and pondered: "What is man that thou art mindful of him ... " David seemed to be filled with the deep longing to know WHY? Why, God, do You care for man; why are You mindful of him? Some would insist that God does not intend for men to know or understand His purposes, and they would recite the words of Isaiah 55:9 as proof: "For as the heavens are higher than the earth, so are my ways higher than your ways, and my thoughts (purposes) than your thoughts." But this does not mean that God limits man; it merely reminds us that God does not allow man to discover these ways or purposes *by his own searching*. There are many facts and bits of knowledge which man can acquire by search and discovery, but God reserves for Himself the giving of *full-knowledge by revelation*.

d Have you ever met the theologian who has spent a life-time searching through his vast library? In his years of research he has moved beyond the WHY to a study of WHO God really is in His Person. But he has become absorbed in his delight for searching out the attributes of God—His righteousness, holiness, unchangeableness, etc. In all this pre-occupation with more and more knowledge about God, you have an inexplainable sense that he has also fallen into, perhaps, the most subtle snare. He has spent his life in a dedication to know more and more *about God* and WHO He really is in His Person, yet you sense a lack in his life. He has knowledge that could fill libraries, yet Paul would insist "he is ever learning and has missed the full-knowledge of THE TRUTH." Why has this happened? To proceed further into the inner-most circle demands a measure of honesty he has been unwilling to give. To know God objectively—is learning more and more; to know God subjectively means to come into a living participation; it means to experience God in the Spirit in a most vital and living way.

e Dr. A. W. Tozer explained this inner-most participation in the reality of God in these words: "God happens to you." By this he meant there was a transmission of divine reality to your life and spirit which utterly transcended words to describe. "God happens to you ... " In that experience you knew you had passed beyond knowing the works, or the ways, or the purpose or the person of God. You had entered into a living reality. Henceforth you were participating in Him. One who has tasted of this participation can understand why Dr. Tozer insisted there was a difference between mere truths and THE TRUTH. "In their search for facts men have confused truths with TRUTH. The words of Christ, Ye shall know THE TRUTH, and the truth shall make you free, have been wrenched from their context and used to stir people to the pursuit of knowledge of many kinds with the expectation of being made free by knowledge. Certainly this is not what Christ had in mind when He uttered the words. Such truths as men discover in the earth beneath and in the astronomic heavens above are properly not truths, but facts. We call them truths, as I do here, but they are no more than parts of the jigsaw puzzle of the universe, and when correctly fitted together they provide at least a hint of what the vast picture is like. But I repeat, they are not truth, and more important, they are not *the truth.* Were every missing piece discovered and laid in place we would still not have the truth, for the truth is not a composite of thoughts and things. The truth should be spelled with a capital T, for it is nothing less than the Son of God, the Second Person of the blessed Godhead." (From an editoral in the ALLIANCE WITNESS)

Finally we can appreciate what Paul meant by THE TRUTH in 2 Tim. 3:7. If men are ever learning and not able to come to the full-knowledge of THE TRUTH, it is because someplace they have become satisfied with mere knowledge. Above all we must clearly understand that it is not necessary to press from the outer through the various circles to the inner-most by a long devious pathway of search, obedience and patience. On the contrary, we must see how God has planned for us to come immediately into an intimate participation in full reality as we live and move and have our being "in Christ." It is no wonder then, that the Chinese use the same word for *truth* and *reality.* To live "in Him" is to live in THE TRUTH, which is in the fullness of divine reality. Now we must see —(on the next page) what it means to live IN HIS VIEW-POINT where we see not mere fragments of His works, His ways, His purposes or His person—but we enjoy the thrill of seeing them all in full-knowledge.

WE CAN NOW APPRECIATE THE ULTIMATE PHILOSOPHY

It was in his letter to the Colossians that Paul warned against that human philosophy which is after the tradition of men. What a snare it is for men to love wisdom, to learn more and more just for knowledge sake. Satan is little concerned when any man is learning about the works, the ways, the purpose and the person of God. That is one thing, but it is quite another thing to "see" as with spiritual eyes. Satan greatly fears when men move into inward illumination where all these things become living and there is a participation in their reality. He knows that in this illumined "seeing" there is a built-in power which implements and things become living and operative.

We can better understand Paul's earnest prayer in their behalf. Instead of being on the outside looking in, he prays that they may—so to speak—be on the inside with God looking out.

GOD'S WAY OF SHARING FULL-KNOWLEDGE

"We are asking God that YOU MAY SEE THINGS, as it were, FROM HIS POINT OF VIEW by being given spiritual insight and understanding. We also pray that your outward lives, which men see, may bring credit to your Master's Name, and that you may bring joy to His heart by bearing genuine Christian fruit, and that your knowledge of God may grow yet deeper. As you live this NEW LIFE, we pray that you will be strengthened from God's boundless resources, so that you will find yourselves able to pass through any experience and endure it with courage. You will even be able to thank God in the midst of pain and distress because you are privileged to share the lot of those who are LIVING IN THE LIGHT" (Col 1:9-12 J. B. Phillips).

Here is the difference. Paul is not preaching a philosophy, but rather a glorious position in Christ whereby all the essential elements automatically become operative in this new life.

(1)   It is not something mental, but something living. He says: "this new life we live."

(2)   As we have pictured in the diagram, we are not on the outside looking in—with mere knowledge; we are "in Him" on the inside looking out. There is a "seeing" which has been made possible by our union in His death, burial, resurrection and positioning in heavenly places.

(3)   We do not have knowledge or wisdom through our own searching. Paul says that in God's viewpoint "we are given spiritual insight and understanding."

(4)   In this glorious participation "in Him" we enjoy seeing all things whole as perfectly related to Him and His intention. Instead of mere fragments we see and rejoice in His works, His ways, His purpose and His person. Yes, from the inside looking out things are so different.

(5)   Finally, we have more than a philosophy; we have "in Christ" the power to perform. Others see this fruitage in our outward lives and it becomes a glorious testimony of reality. Thus He lives His life in us, and in this NEW LIFE we are strengthened by His resources, triumphant no matter what comes.

THIS IS THE ULTIMATE PHILOSOPHY GOD INTENDS

THE

ULTIMATE

ISSUE IN LIFE

ALL CREATION FULFILLS
HIS PURPOSE EXCEPT---!

DESIGNED TO
EXPRESS HIS LIFE:

THAT WHICH IS MERELY RELATED
TO MAN-CANNOT BE ULTIMATE

WHAT IS THE ULTIMATE
ISSUE IN LIFE?

ALL CREATION FULFILLS
HIS PURPOSE EXCEPT---!

ONE BEAUTIFUL MORNING a very strange conversation took place in the woods. While there were many who looked on and listened, there were just four voices heard to speak. A tiny white lily waved in the breeze by the trickling stream. High above her towered the branches of a gnarled old oak tree.

"Are you not ashamed of yourself, little flower," exclaimed the mighty oak. "When you see how big I am, do you not feel insignificant; while my branches spread far out in every direction, you fill such a small space in this world."

"No," replied the lily. "We are both just what God made us. And to each of us He has given a gift: fragrance to me and strength to you."

"Where will your sweetness be a few days from now?" asked the oak scornfully. "You will soon wither and decay, and your grave will not lift the ground higher by a blade of grass. But I shall live on for years—perhaps even for centuries. And when I am cut down, I may be built into a mighty ship to carry men over the sea; or perhaps I shall be fashioned into a coffin that will hold the body of a prince or a king. Ah, little frail lily, what is your lot in comparison to mine?"

Now while the oak was taunting the lily, a little brown squirrel sitting on the lowest branch of the oak had been most attentive to their conversation. Indeed he was quite impressed by the boasting of the mighty oak, but he was equally alert to the gentle confidence of the little lily as it spoke to the oak.

"It is true," replied the lily humbly, "that I am small and frail, and that I shall not live long. But if I live fragrantly I shall have added my small bit of beauty and enjoyment to the world. I shall then have filled the complete purpose of the One who sent me—my Creator; and that is all that really matters to me."

Just then another listening ear could hold her voice no longer. It was the tiny raindrop whose voice burst forth announcing: "Please do not think me rude if I intrude, for indeed I am smallest of all; so very, very small beside the oak, yes, even small beside the lily or the squirrel. But I am sure I have learned the wondrous secret of living."

The tiny raindrop knew that every ear was tuned, for all were interested in knowing this secret. So she began, "When I am sent by my Creator on my long journey down to earth, I approach with just one thing in view: to fulfill His purpose in sending me. Oh mighty oak, my life seems so very short as I wash your leaves and bark, and soak your thirsty roots. Oh little squirrel, I love to wash your glossy coat of fur and, perchance, even to quench your inner thirst. Oh, lovely lily, I always hope that I can fall upon you to freshen and release your gracious fragrance. I love to be near you, for you also seem so content with fulfilling our Creator's purpose. That must be why you are always looking up to HIM."

At last the little squirrel was fully convinced, and it was time for him to speak: "Oh mighty oak, beside you, I, too, have always felt so very insignificant until this morning. Suddenly I remembered that many, many generations ago one of my family planted a small acorn from which you grew. Is it not wonderful that our Creator placed this instinct within my breast that I too might fulfill His purpose in my being?"

That morning as the meeting broke up, you could hear the mighty oak leading every member of the forest in this triumphant chorus: HOW WONDERFUL TO BE ALIVE, ESPECIALLY WHEN YOU ARE ALIVE TO FULFILLING THE CREATOR'S PURPOSE.

LIFE'S THREE-FOLD SECRET UNFOLDS

Perhaps this little fantasy will help us probe into life's three-fold secret. Really all the important issues of life are wrapped up in God and in knowing...

> why He has sent us,
> how He has designed us to function,
> when He is satisfied with our life.

How amazing it might be if the whole inanimate creation could actually talk to us. Yet there is a sense in which it does talk—even as these voices in the woods have just spoken to us. How emphatically they seem to remind us that all things have been created by God and sent forth to fulfill some distinctive existence. But the oak, the lily, the raindrop and the squirrel are like mere puppets who must necessarily reflect God's glory, for they are without moral choice. Since they cannot actually ponder their origin, function or purpose, they cannot enjoy the same God-consciousness which man has been uniquely designed to enjoy. The power to appreciate, to enjoy, to sense satisfaction is reserved for man who alone posesses the soul faculties of mind, emotion and will. Nor can the inanimate creation understand its nature or inward makeup; it just functions according to built-in laws of nature in fulfilling its short span of existence.

It is true when man comes forth from the creative hand of God, he already has a certain "built-in-mechanism" which functions quite naturally in his being. Having this soul mechanism he is far above the brute creation. But wait! God has uniquely designed another part of man that he might receive a whole new set of "built-ins"—a whole new spiritual mechanism which operates on an entirely different frequency than the soul. Thus God made man with a human spirit which is so designed that it can live with a continual God-consciousness—a sense of divine commission which the raindrop was picturing for us, a sense of proper function which the lily was describing, a sense of fully satisfying God—as these lived merely to realize His intention.

Now the great difficulty in most of God's children is, that they try to know the fulfilling of this three-fold secret with either their physical or soul mechanism. Neither the body nor the soul have been designed by God for this special function of God-consciousness. This is why the majority of God's children fall into despair and finally assume one cannot know whether he is satisfying God. What is wrong? They are using the wrong built-in mechanism, not the one which God wants to install and make operative.

Is it too much of a fantasy—too unreal to insist that everyone should (even as we have pictured the lily and raindrop) approach life and all things with this overshadowing consciousness: that they know God has sent them into life with a specific mission to fulfill; that they know the proper function of their spirit, soul and body as God intended; that they know—even as Enoch of old seems to have known—that they please God and He is satisfied with their walk, devotion and dedication?

Oh dear reader, be sure that some "Big Oak" will try to overwhelm you and scorn your deepest longing to make this three-fold secret operative. Just remember that every Big Oak who lives "in the woods" where things are not always bright and clear is prone to evaluate things after the soul. All the man-of-soul can ever do is compare others with himself; but the one who is inwardly exercised in his spirit enjoys a continual God-consciousness, knowing an inward sense of proper function, knowing a sense of divine destiny being fulfilled.

This is the ultimate issue in life. Shall we listen to the Big Oak and continue to flounder in the dark shadows of life, or shall we tune in to hear the One who made the Big Oak—and discover life's full and true meaning?

Whoever has truly uncovered this secret, can be assured he is enjoying the fulness of living with divine meaning and ultimate perspective. The following articles of this journal have been selected or written to aid in the unfolding of this secret.

THE FATHER has purposed that all things should find their meaning and value in Christ ......

BUT WHEN MAN interprets life as related to himself it looks like this ....

All, Backwards, Despair, Frustration, etc.... Confusion, Emptiness,

HE alone makes sense of life

CHRIST, AS ALPHA AND OMEGA, makes sense of life. I might have a tray with all the letters of any alphabet jumbled up in it. If I know what the letters are, and I know what I want, I can put them in an order so that they make sense. They express exactly what I want to express. All that comes between "A" and "Z", between Alpha and Omega, makes sense when it is put in its right place. There are many people today who cannot make sense of life at all. The struggle of many is to try to make sense of life: What does it all mean? What is the explanation of it all? It seems all a jumble, a confusion, an enigma. Jesus makes sense of life: He puts the jumble into proper order.

That is the description of the Divine design, the great purpose of God: to provide an explanation of everything. Yes, in Him we have the answer to our life's problems; in Him we have the setting in order of lives disrupted and confused. Has that not been true of so many whose lives were all mixed up and confused, distorted and twisted, without any seeming design or pattern, meaning or explanation; they could not make sense of anything.

And then they came to the Lord Jesus, and life made sense: a design, a pattern came in, and they came to realize what it all meant, what they were for. That is the testimony of those who are truly His. In the Lord Jesus, we have found a pattern, a design for life: we have found a meaning in life, an explanation of life. He alone can bring into life a clear pattern, a new understanding. In Him, as Alpha and Omega, we have all that we need to make sense.

Let me repeat: Until you have your letters, your basic characters, there is no beginning, and there will be no sensible, meaningful end at all. Jesus just supplies that need—a beginning and a sensible end. He leads somewhere! When you and I at last reach the end, the end in glory, it will truly be a meaningful end, will it not? It will be an end that justifies everything, that gives meaning to everything, that explains everything. The thousand 'why's' of life-time will be answered, will all be explained. Why this experience and that? why this sorrow and that? why this disappointment and that loss? why these strange ways in our life? It will all be answered in the end—and Jesus Himself will be the End! Yes, it will be a 'sensible' end. We shall have no quarrel with God then, because Jesus will have put it all straight, and brought us to an end beyond our wildest expectations and altogether beyond our merits.

CHRIST alone can give · · ·   Z

                                        Finisher,
                              Energizer
                    Designer,
            Creator,
      Beginner,
Author,

                    meaning and order to life

OUR CONFIDENCE IS ALSO IN HIS FINISHING . . . .

And Christ is the Last, the Omega, the end—in this sense, that, when He begins a thing, He finishes it. "The Lord will perfect that which concerns us" (Ps. 118:8). "He which began a good work in you will perfect it until the day of Jesus Christ" (Phil 1:6). He finishes what He begins. And He is not only the Beginner and the Perfecter, but Himself the Beginning and the Ending—the Finish. God is working all things to the end that we should be "conformed to the image of His Son" (Rom. 8:29). Christ stands so to speak, right at the end: and God is moving and working in us, His people, in relation to that One who stands at the end, that we should be conformed to His image. The servant of God cries: "I shall be satisfied, when I awake, with thy likeness" (Psa. 17:15). It is that likeness that is the end: Jesus Himself is the End. All things under Heaven's government are working towards conformity to God's Son. — T.A.S.

WHY DOES HUMANITY EXIST?

Norman Grubb answers:

"NOT TO BECOME SOMETHING, BUT TO CONTAIN SOMEONE"

WHEN I WENT TO the Congo as a young missionary, I faced a very real question to which I sought an answer. What had I really to take to those people? What had I in myself?

Mind you, I was an earnest young missionary. I was not short of consecration. I was not short of commitment. I had a continuing prayer and Bible-reading life. Jesus Christ had become my Savior. I knew that my life was to be Jesus Christ to other people. And yet I didn't have what it took; I had the wrong idea of life. It became necessary to have some reorientations of my understanding of things.

My concept of life had become distorted because I had been thinking, "There is love and faith and power and holiness in the Bible, and I'm sure God will kind of impart it to me somehow, so that I will become a loving person, a believing person, a powerful person." I could not see for the life of me but that I should become something.

This, then, was the first and greatest problem: a misunderstanding of what life is. I think we all start there. It is really a product of the fall: We interpret life as something that we live ourselves; so that even when we become born again of God's Spirit, and saved through the Grace of our Lord Jesus Christ, we still interpret life as something we are living now. We have a job to do, a home to run, and so we seek to live a life in contact with God through Jesus Christ, so we can get assistance and guidance and leadership from Him.

I had to discover that this was not life at all, rather that life is a total reverse of it. Life is not an assistance or an addition; it is a replacement. There is only one Person who really lives in the whole universe, and that is the living God Himself. He is the One who is the Three, who is self-giving love. He is the One who is the love of the universe. And we humans exist that we may be means by which He expresses Himself. Humanity itself exists to express Deity.

In order to get that into focus, I had to go through stages of destruction, making room for construction. The initial stage, of course, is when we at last face the fact that we are sinners. We recognize that we are cut off from God, and that there is something that He did which we could not do, when He came in the Person of Jesus Christ and wiped out all the consequences of our sin with the shedding of His precious blood.

When we come to Him we do not receive a past option, we receive a present Person who died for us. He comes into our hearts and there is born a love for Him that is not our love. The proof that we are redeemed is that the love in our hearts for Jesus Christ is greater than our love for ourselves.

But because of the false concept of life that we have, even though we are born anew we still tend to think, "Now we have the Lord Jesus Christ. We shall live for Him and work for Him." So once again we have to go down, not up, to learn another great lesson. We human selves do not do what we should do—that is true. But it is equally true that we human selves *cannot* do what we should do. We have to discover not only our guilt but our helplessness.

WE COME TO A SECOND CRASH

As unredeemed sinners we come face to face with our guilt and our lost condition. As redeemed new men we have to discover our helplessness; so that instead of counting ourselves able to live the Christian life and to do the kind of good we ought, we find ourselves positively unable. So we have to come to a second crash.

The first crash found us guilty sinners; the second crash finds us helpless saints, and it is a crash that is more difficult to recognize. I must come to a place where I find that life is not *I* living it, with God's assistance and His partnership; rather it is *He,* an entirely other Person, living it, and I am the means by which He lives it as a replacement.

The simple surprise that God gave me in Africa was contained in the little phrase in the Bible, "God is love." I saw that John was not saying "God *has* love," but "God *is* love." There is a big difference. If you *have* a thing, it is not you. I have a coat on my back, and if I take it off and give it to you, I am still here. Thus the New Testament does not teach that God has a thing called love which He gives to you. It says, "God is love."

If that be true, then love is a Person. If God is love, the only self-giving love in the universe is one exclusive Person. It is not what He has and gives you, it is something that He is. He is not a Person who gives something, but rather One who *is* something.

I began studying further. I wanted power, and I discovered that the Bible teaches that Christ is the power of God. Not that Christ *has* the power, and utilizes it. He powers a person because He is the Person; and all powers are manifestations of this one Person.

I came also to study the word "life." We often speak of "having" eternal life. But I find that Jesus did not say, "I have the life and give

179

it to you." He says, "I am the Life." Life is a Person. I came to the end of my pursuit when I found the little expression in Colossians 3:11, "Now Christ is all, and in all." And there I discovered the reverse of my outlook on life.

I suddenly saw that the reason for the existence of humanity is not to become something, but to contain Someone. Not to become something built up by hard work; that is where our strains and stresses and guilt and condemnation arise. We are ashamed of ourselves; we ask, "Why am I not better?" We think that we ought to be changed, but we never change. What we receive is a new Person inside of us—which is quite a different thing.

To become something means that I have to be built up. To contain something means that the container doesn't matter, but what it contains is important. Thus the New Testament gives us the A-B-C of living the Christian life: it tells us that we are to be vessels. "Vessel" is a very simple and humbling word. A vessel has no other reason for existing than its capacity to contain. It can just be a cup or a pot.

THE END OF MY PURSUIT

The basic lesson for time or eternity that we as humans are to learn is that we are vessels capable of containing God. The distortion of life that we got as a consequence of the fall makes it appear that life is "activity." We like to live, to use our minds and wills. But the truth is that the secret of life is not activity, it is receptivity. Activity is only a product of receptivity.

God is the invisible Person, the only real Person in the universe. He is the love, the life, the wisdom, the all; but being an invisible Person, He must have a means of manifestation. The whole universe manifests Him and shows forth His glory, but God is still a Person. And you cannot see a person just in light, or in music, or in color. You can see something of him, but you cannot see that he is a person.

So God created persons to express His own Person by them. The basic purpose of us human beings therefore should be to become the vessels that contain Him. That means our permanent habit has to become receptivity rather than activity.

Love always makes it as easy as it can. God is love, and He has made humanity as easy as He can. If life is not easy for us, it is because we are not quite right yet. And the easiest possible function a person can conceive of is the function of receptivity. You just receive what is poured on you; you just take it. Nothing else.

If you look at nature, you see that a tree does not produce one leaf by activity. Vegetation receives. It has sunlight and moisture poured on it. What it receives it uses, but activity is only a product of receptivity. Thus did I begin to learn the basic secret of life.

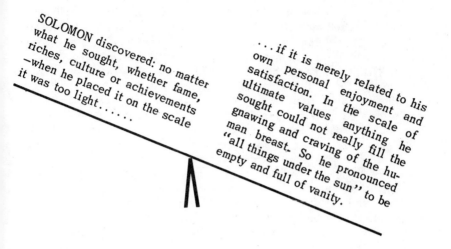

SOLOMON discovered: no matter what he sought, whether fame, riches, culture or achievements —when he placed it on the scale it was too light......

... if it is merely related to his own personal enjoyment and satisfaction. In the scale of ultimate values anything he sought could not really fill the gnawing and craving of the human breast. So he pronounced "all things under the sun" to be empty and full of vanity.

THAT WHICH IS MERELY RELATED
TO MAN—CANNOT BE ULTIMATE

PERHAPS no living man has ever possessed as much as King Solomon. In his greatest hour he had wisdom, knowledge, fame, riches, servants, great achievements, wives and cultural arts. But in evaluating all this he tells us: "Whatsoever my eyes desired I kept not from them, I withheld not my heart from any joy...then I looked on all the works that my hands had wrought, and...behold all was VANITY AND VEXATION OF SPIRIT...."

Is not this God's most graphic way of proving to all mankind the utter futility and emptiness of all that "this world has to offer." What could a natural heart crave that Solomon did not have? Over and over again throughout the book of Ecclesiastes we are reminded all this is simply one man's desperate conclusion as he sees things "under the sun." Everything that could bring enjoyment and satisfaction turns out to be empty and meaningless. Why? There must be some reason?

From the beginning of this journal we have sought to establish one premise: only as the issues of life are properly related to God can we appreciate why we are here on this earth. It is proper relatedness that gives meaning, value, purpose and significance to life. Just for a moment consider that life comes in four dimensions and you will see how this must be true:

FIRST, what is the value of great *length of life*, if it has not been related to fulfilling the purpose God intends. To prolong life is merely a torture when its meaning has slipped. Last week I stood in the hospital by the side of a sweet little lady. She sobbed and cried out to God to take her home and away from such intense suffering—unless, unless He could fulfill something in all this. Unless her days could be related to HIM, they were more than meaningless; they were sheer torture.

SECOND, there is the breadth of life or *how interestingly we live.* But who can find a true devotion to life? Our devotion must be to the One who has given life. Throughout his days it seems as though Solomon is ever grasping for this devotion which will give interest to life. There is no inconvenience he would not suffer. There is no hardship he would not endure. There is no expense he would not involve himself in if it would just give life that proper devotion. But because he saw life only in relatedness to himself—it was empty and without interest. How different are the words of the apostle Paul who seems to have discovered the secret of right relatedness: "For me to live is Christ," I hear him insist. Paul would be the first to explain how Christ gave breadth, for in every hour there was something new, something challenging and ultimate on the horizon.

THIRD, there is the depth of life or *how intensely we live.* Solomon seems to represent a man who lived "all out." When he saw something he wanted, he expended every energy to achieve that thing. He was a man of intense dedication: "...whatever my eyes desired I kept not from them, ... " But herein we see the futility of man's dedication to his own pursuits. God's way is to move us out of our own into His stream of dedication. To be cut loose, detached from our own intensity of living and find ourselves alive only to HIS DEDICATION; that, is the proper relatedness in this dimension we call depth. Almost every week I smile at one of my close friends. As he wipes away the sweat from his brow I remind him again and again, "I've seldom watched a man with such intense dedication; friend, you're eaten up with zeal—but what is it accomplishing in the scales of eternal values?" He only smiles and continues his torturous pace. To him it seems I am also "eaten up with zeal to achieve an objective." But I believe the difference is that I live in the flow of His zeal. Then it is not ours, for we move with a sense of finality. It is not our zeal but his zeal; "... the zeal of the Lord of hosts shall perform this.

FOURTH, there is that dimension which might correspond more or less to the peculiar fourth dimension in space which is the purpose of life or *why we live.* Who can properly grasp this dimension until God helps one to see from His own vantage point. Solomon tried to explain it thus: "He has made everything beautiful in its time; He also has planted eternity in men's heart and mind (a divinely implanted sense of a purpose working through the ages which nothing under the sun, but only God, can satisfy), yet so that man cannot find out what God has done from the beginning to the end" (Eccles. 3:11 A.N.T). Surely 'his is the best conclusing of Solomon. He confesses to that mysterious gnawing in his breast. Oh that he might fulfill his purpose in being. And it is true that no man by searching can ever find out "what God has done from the beginning to the end." But wait! That does not mean God cannot unveil this purpose to one! Man's futile searching is one thing; but God's desire to reveal to those who are pure in heart is yet something else. "...the pure in heart shall see..." See what? There is no limitation with God; for He will share with man all that he can profitably receive. Once again we see how this fourth dimension of life's purpose— like all the other dimensions—takes on meaning only as related to God.

| When our life is totally related to Him in all four dimensions... | ..then we live for His pleasure and satisfaction; and living in Him—we also enjoy all with Him. |

Finally, let us turn away from Solomon to a man who seems to have discovered how to relate everything to God. It is Moses who starts that glorious 90th Psalm with this anthem of proper relatedness:

"Lord, You have been our dwelling place and our refuge in all generations (says Moses). Before the mountains were brought forth, or ever You had formed and given birth to the earth and the world, even from everlasting to everlasting YOU ARE GOD" (Psalm 90:1-2 A.N.T.).

Here is a man who has "seen" with the help of the Spirit how all things have their source and relatedness to God. Moses tells us of his dwelling place—of his continual viewpoint in the very heart of God. *This was his secret!* So just a few verses later (vs 12) it is quite meaningful when he pleads:

"So teach us to number our days that we may apply our hearts unto wisdom." The word translated "number" is "manah" in the original and comes from the root meaning "to WEIGH." We may therefore read the verse, "Teach us to place each day in the balance"; or, "teach us to weigh each day's achievements on the scale of ultimate values." How long we live is not nearly so important as how meaningfully we pass our days; how broad our life reaches out is not nearly so important as how much value it fulfills for God; how deep we send our roots down is not important if those roots are not "in Him"—and His dedication; how purposefully we live is not significant if we have not found ourselves in the stream of HIS PURPOSE.

ONE HAS SHARED THIS TESTIMONY:

For years I assumed that my life could show forth God's glory by allowing Him to perform some miraculous feat or accomplish some outstanding work through me. I wanted to exhibit His power, might and authority in some spectacular way. I see now that all this while He has been waiting to exhibit His beautiful character in the routine and common-place experiences of life. No wonder I have been frustrated. I had my own expectation of how to show forth His glory and it was quite different from the way He had planned. What a change has come since I discovered . . . . .

How to Fulfill Life's Higest Purpose

O NE GREAT PURPOSE of the incarnation was that here, on earth, the Lord Jesus should show men what God is like. This was a task committed to Him by the Father, and in His last great prayer He was able to hand back that trust as completed—'having accomplished that which Thou gavest Me to do'. We are left in no doubt as to what was being considered, for He Himself explained it by saying, "I have glorified thee on the earth". This does not seem to refer to His atoning death, for the words were spoken before He was crucified; it seems rather to speak of His daily life here on the earth, here among men. On this same earth on which we live and in similar human experiences which are common to us all, He was entrusted with the task of displaying the true character of God, and so showing forth the Divine glory. He was given the task, and He could claim fully to have performed it.

OUR LIFE'S WORK

Is it not true that we also have a life-work? Is there not also in our case some task which the Father has given us to do? A great deal of confusion exists about this very matter, with many and varied counsels as to what Christians ought to be doing. When we turn to the Word of God, however, there is no confusion, for the matter is clearly explained in the words, and illustrated in the life of the Son of God. His life's work here on the earth, as a Man, was to glorify the Father. In essence, the same is true in our case: we also are called to glorify God here on earth. Should we desire further enlightenment on this matter, we are given help in the words of the Lord Jesus Himself, who described His successful living by reminding Philip that,"he that hath seen me hath seen the Father". This was at least one phase of Christ's life-work:to demonstrate personally the character of God, and to let men see how that character could be expressed in human experience.

For us, also, the purpose of our redeemed lives here on earth is that the same glorious character should be shown to men—that Christ should be magnified in our bodies. Peter stressed the corporate nature of this revelation, saying that the elect race and royal priesthood of God's people have been chosen "that ye may shew forth the excellencies of him who called you... "(I Pet. ii. 9). In Paul's personal testimony, however, we have the more individual aspect of this same Divine out-shining, and we shall confine what we now have to say to the individual and personal. The words are familiar enough, that "Christ shall be mag-nified in my body, whether by life, or by death." Quite clearly this re-presented the apostle's supreme concern, that which, so far as he was concerned, was the most important thing of all, his "earnest expecta-tion and hope", the meaning of his existence and the cause for which he would gladly lay down his life. It was not just that Christ should be glorified in some general way, or vaguely in unseen realms, but there and then, literally in his own human body, there should be ample proof of the Lord's greatness.

We have used the word 'task'. It should not be thought, however, that anything irksome was involved, or that it was a question of any job of work to be taken up or later laid aside. Christian living repre-sented no burden to him. His was no legal drudgery of what you must or must not do. No, he thankfully claimed to have been delivered from any-thing of that nature. His life now had a rhythm, a meaning and a pur-pose; it had nothing in it of the burdensome or restrictive. On the con-trary, there is much in this letter to the Philippians to prove that it was his sublimest joy, his constant source of heart satisfaction, to have the privilege of living Christ as well as of talking about Him. The words do not refer primarily to his work as a preacher or teacher, to what we so often call 'ministry'. Of course such work is ministry. It is our chief and most important ministry. But the emphasis is not on good works, but on a quality of life.

WRONG IDEAS OF GLORY

We must beware of wrong ideas or expectations when we consider this magnifying of our Lord. We need always to consider Him. There were, of course, events in His public ministry when it was obvious that God's glory was being revealed. When the sea waves, in their tumul-tuous fury, were silenced at a word, then there could be no question about the powerful presence of God. When the Lord Jesus stood at the tomb of Lazarus and with a simple word of command called the dead man back to life and to the outside world, then everyone marvelled, as well they might. There were many such acts of power in the course of Christ's ministry which truly glorified the Father. But it was surely not of these that the Lord was speaking when He affirmed that those who had seen Him had seen the Father. So much of His life was occupied with the simple, ordinary things, the humdrum, the obscure and even the menial, and it was in these daily affairs of human experience that the Lord Jesus claimed to have glorified the Father on earth. So much more of our lives is occupied with these same things: here, then, is a sphere of opportunity in which Christ can be magnified in *our* bodies.

We have our own ideas of glory, and they are often wrong. There was an afternoon when Jesus sat, travel-stained and weary, hungry and thirsty, by the side of Jacob's well. Most people, and many Christians among them, would not consider that such a condition could possibly glorify the Father. They would reason, God is not like that! There were no outward evidences of glory in that dusty Traveller with His simple request for a drink of water from the well. That day He did no sensational miracle. He gave no sign from heaven. Yet in that tired body there was such a manifestation of the Father's grace and goodness that the Samaritan woman became completely transformed. She caught a glimpse of heavenly glories, even though the medium of the vision was the human body of a humble Man tramping along Samaria's dusty highways. Such a story makes us echo the apostle's prayer that 'Christ may also be magnified in my body'.

What a lesson for us, then, not to be striving for that which gratifies *our* idea of what is glorifying to God, but to be content for Him to reveal Himself through us in every circumstance. We must never fall into the mistake of imagining that the circumstances and difficulties of life, the apparent contradictions, the humbling trials or the mundane trivialities, are hindrances to spiritual usefulness, nor to think that only when we are freed from such distractions can we properly fulfil our 'ministry'. No, this is our ministry, as it was Christ's; this is the thing which He has given us to do: to let men see what He is like, for He is always glorious.

ONLY ONE THING MATTERS

For Paul, there was only one consideration worthy of attention, and that was the glorifying of Christ in his body. What happened to him personally was of very small consequence. He did not say, 'I must at all costs live', nor did he say, 'I must on no account die'. Alas! that, so often these and even unworthier selfish considerations are given so much weight! To the apostle, the important thing was not what happened to him, but whether Christ was being magnified while it happened. Prosperity or adversity, comfort or suffering, even life or death—these were not the important alternatives. The really vital question was as to whether, in that human body of his, something of Christ was being revealed, to God's glory, or whether, on the other hand, there was only shameful failure. His concern and his hope was that "in nothing" should there be that in his life which would fail to magnify Christ. Neither he nor we can affirm that those who see us see the Father, or see Christ. There would be an element of presumption, or something worse, if we did. Yet we ought to be able to know that, in seeing us, men see something of Christ. Not only in the great moments of spiritual exaltation, but in the ordinary affairs of our daily existence, people should meet Christ when they meet us.

"For to me to live is Christ" is only possible because Christ Himself lives in me. This, of course, was the secret of the manifestation of the Father's glory in His Son. The Lord Jesus Himself explained His own claim by adding "... the Father in me ... " (John xiv. 10, 11). It was not that He was trying to give them an exhibition, to demonstrate something which would give people an impression of what the Father was like. It was the Father abiding in Him who did the works. And how else can we show men what Christ is like? The secret for us is the same as the secret of Christ's fulfilled task—it is the secret of the indwelling.

There was a "supply of the Spirit of Jesus Christ" for Paul, and that made it possible for Christ to be magnified in him. It was a supply which was always available, but only appreciated and appropriated as and when the apostle came to know his need. Life is meant to bring a succession of discoveries of our need of Christ, and with every such discovery the way is opened for a new inflow of the supply. This is the explanation of so much that we cannot otherwise understand—this plunging of us into new tests where only a fresh supply of the Spirit of Jesus Christ will meet our need. And as our need is met, as we prove the sufficiency of Christ to meet our own inward need, so there can be a new showing forth of His glory through us.

The supply is also described as the answer to the supplications of praying friends. We often do not know how best to pray for one another. The Philippians found this difficulty in the case of Paul. It seems that they had prayed for his release from prison, and so were perplexed, because it looked as though their prayers had not been answered. But they had. True, he was not released from prison, but that was not the real objective of their praying. That objective was—or at least should have been—that Christ might be magnified in Paul's body. And there is abundant reason for believing that, in spite of the prison, or perhaps better because of the prison. Christ was magnified in him. "As always ... " were his words. It may be in preaching, it may be in silence; it may be by mighty works or it may be by terrible sufferings; by life or by death, what matters, so long as the glory of Christ is seen in him?

There is, of course, one great difference between the Lord Jesus and all others. In our case—even in the case of an apostle Paul—there is our own old life which will always obscure the Lord's glory if it is given the opportunity. If people meet *me*, they will not meet the Lord. It may be a nice 'me' or it may be an unpleasant 'me', but if they only meet me I shall have failed of my life's vocation and they will get no true blessing. Our consolation is that the Spirit who supplies our new inward life is also the Spirit who can make real in us the delivering work of the Cross. When self is dealt with by the Cross, when faith lays hold of the abundant supply of the Spirit, then, and then only, can Christ be magnified in our bodies, and we also accomplish that which the Father has given us to do.　　　H. F.

Jesus Said to Mary:　"One thing is needful!"

Paul Said:　"... This one thing I do ..."

David Said:　"... One thing have I desired..."

WHAT IS THE ULTIMATE ISSUE IN LIFE?

THESE STATEMENTS quoted above point our thinking to this question: what is the one imperative thing—above all other things—most needful in life? The answer we give to this question is most revealing. As we shall see, it uncovers our heart attitude toward life, unveils our purpose in living, describes our highest conception of God and reveals our relationship to Him.

What answers do we get? The ordinary man of the street will almost invariably reply: "For me, the one most needful thing is to find happiness and the fullest enjoyment of life." Another who has allowed some small impact of religion upon his life will quote: "Let us hear the conclusion of the whole matter: Fear God, and keep His commandments: for this is the whole duty of man" (Ecc. 12:13). But such answers will not satisfy many believers. They will hasten to correct: "Oh no, the one most needful thing in life is to be "born again." Others will add: "and be momentarily ready for the rapture."

Again, I recall an elderly woman whose testimony in church one evening revealed her limited conception of life's true purpose when she said: "My highest aim is to make heaven my home." What was more alarming, the great majority in that congregation seemed to give unanimous consent: this was also their highest goal in life!

But with Mary, with Paul or with David, there was something much higher, something much more ultimate which was the imperative issue in life. Each of their statements seem to carry the very same undertone. Though on the surface each statement refers to something quite different, yet there is the same atunement to the ultimate pitch.

First, it seems quite clear that with Mary, with Paul or David the *one thing most needful* was not personal salvation from sin or hell, it was not the new birth, nor even to be separated from this world and be completely submissive unto God. However good and necessary these may be, every fallen son of Adam has one greater need which includes all of these lesser needs. Man needs, above all else, to see himself related to God for His pleasure, glory and satisfaction. There are thousands sitting in church pews every Sunday who would quickly testify to all that God has done *for them,* but just here they fall short of their greatest need. They have missed this most needful rectification which would relate them to God for Himself.

It is not enough to see God and His working related to our welfare and blessing. When Calvary has accomplished its deepest, most thorough explosion within us, we begin to cry out with the Apostle Paul, "THIS ONE THING I DO. . ." What was this? He was reaching forth, "pressing toward" the fulfillment and realization in his life of that for which God had uniquely marked him out. Paul seems utterly overmastered with this ONE THING: That God may find pleasure and satisfaction in him through the fulfillment of this high calling. With Paul we conclude the *ultimate issue in life* is that realization which satisfies HIM. He was completely God-related.

Second, it seems that Mary, Paul and David had found: *how* life's true meaning and fulfillment could be realized. Since they must be related to Him, for Himself—not merely for their own blessing and enjoyment—*how* could this satisfaction of God's heart be accomplished? Jesus saw Mary sitting at His feet. In her giving attention, giving devotion, giving herself to Him, she was concerned primarily for His highest pleasure, His satisfaction—not her own. Martha was of course giving her time, her labors and her service for Him, yet Jesus insists: "Mary hath chosen that better part." Mary was not giving something— but rather, was giving herself to Him. How much more satisfying to Him!

Third, when we are truly fulfilling the *one thing most needful*, there is a full satisfaction for God, but there is also a participation by us in that divine satisfaction. What is not sought *by us* is shared *with us*. This wonderful way of receiving and giving is the divine rule of action.

Consider then, how David desired ". . . to dwell . . . to behold . . ., to enquire . . ." (Ps. 27). At first reading it may appear that David's desire was quite centered in his own welfare and enjoyment. For those who insist thus, we would agree that David, then, needed a rectifying in his desires. But it is also possible that David was more alive to pleasing the Lord than himself. He well knew that we are made for God. There are too many outbursts of praise and exaltation when he "blesses the Lord" and rejoices in HIS benefits, i.e. what God receives, for us to believe that David is primarily interested in "dwelling in His house, beholding His beauty and enquiring—all' for his own satisfaction.

No, it would seem to us that David desires all of this to bring satisfaction to God. There is a depth of meaning which must not elude us. In our delighting, God is delighted; in our being satisfied—God is satisfied. It works both ways in a mutual satisfaction. I prefer to believe this is what David would teach us in announcing so boldly: "One thing have I desired. . . ." It is what Paul is echoing: "This one thing I do. . . ." It is what Jesus is telling Mary: "One thing is needful. . . ." And we are being caught with the same yearning:

> Oh, to belong to Thee,
> > Just for Thyself;
> To find all our delights,
> > In delighting Thy Heart!
> To press for the goal;
> > Of satisfying Thee,
> To have full, fulfilled,
> > That ONE THING MOST NEEDFUL.